COOPERATIVE
LEARNING
ACROSS THE CURRICULUM

Cynthia Rothman

Troll Associates

Metric Conversion Chart

1 inch = 2.54 cm

1 foot = .305 m

1 yard = .914 m

1 mile = 1.61 km

1 square mile = 2.6 square km

1 fluid ounce = 29.573 ml

1 dry ounce = 28.35 g

1 ton = .91 metric ton

1 gallon = 3.79 l

1 pound = 0.45 kg

1 cup = .24 l

1 pint = .473 l

1 teaspoon = 4.93 ml

1 tablespoon = 14.78 ml

Conversion from Fahrenheit to
Celsius: subtract 32 and then
multiply the remainder by 5/9.

Interior Illustrations by Mary Gwen Connolly

ISBN: 0-8167-3269-8

Printed in the United States of America
10 9 8 7 6 5 4 3 2 1

Table of Contents

Introduction v

A Cooperative Learning Classroom

Introducing Cooperative Learning..............7
Working Together: Primary 8
Partners All! (reproducible) 9
Can You Find Us? (reproducible)...............10
Partners' Team-Up Sheet (reproducible) 11
Working Together: Intermediate...............12
Prefix Pursuit..12
Terrific Teammates! (reproducible)............14
Team-Up Sheet (reproducible)...................15
Guide's Job Sheet (reproducible) 16
Recorder's Job Sheet (reproducible) 17
Checker's Job Sheet (reproducible) 18
Booster's Job Sheet (reproducible) 19
Organizer's Job Sheet (reproducible).........20
Reporter's Job Sheet (reproducible) 21
How Did It Go? 22
Keeping Track.......................................22
Helpful Hints..23
Keeping Track:
    Primary (reproducible) 24
Keeping Track:
    Intermediate (reproducible)..................25
Just Rewards (reproducible) 26
Perfect Partners Award (reproducible).......27
Terrific Team Award (reproducible) 28

Primary Activities

Reading/Language Arts
Create a Treat..29
Come Share a Book!................................30
Mystery Rhyme Time...............................31
What Could It Be? 32
What Could It Be? (reproducible) 33
Once Upon a Time 34
Once Upon a Time (reproducible).............35

Science
Does Your Boat Float?.............................36
Does Your Boat Float? (reproducible) 37
Using Your Senses..................................38

Using Your Senses (reproducible) 39
In a Prehistoric Zoo 40
Starry, Starry Night................................41

Math
At the Toy Shop.....................................42
At the Toy Shop (reproducible)...................43
Inch by Inch...44
Yours and Mine 45
Picture This! 46
Picture This! (reproducible) 47
Pattern a Pattern 48

Social Studies
Where Am I? 49
Safety First! 50
Safety First! (reproducible) 51
Make a Map 52
Make a Map (reproducible) 53
What Will We Bring? 54
A Neighborhood Museum 55

Art
A Paintbox of Our Own 56
A Paintbox of Our Own (reproducible) 57
Sand Art 58
Stencil Fun..59
Imagine That!..60
Imagine That! (reproducible) 61
Playful Pets...62

Intermediate Activities

Reading/Language Arts
At the Card Shop 63
Think Thesaurus! 64
Think Thesaurus! (reproducible) 65
Invent a Game.......................................66
Invent a Game (reproducible)....................67
As... As... 68
Our Dream Catalog 69

Science
Believe It or Not! 70

Believe It or Not! (reproducible) 71
Recycling Reminders 72
Animal, Vegetable, or Mineral? 73
Are You an Amphibian? 74
Are You an Amphibian? (reproducible) 75

Math

Measure Up 76
Measure Up (reproducible) 77
Amazing Mazes 78
Code and Decode 79
Collectors All 80
Collectors All (reproducible) 81
Best Jelly Bean Contest Ever 82

Social Studies

Rain Forest Treasure 83
The Great State of ____ 84
The Great State of ____ (reproducible) 85
Time Line Mix-Ups 86
Time Line Mix-Ups (reproducible) 87
Tales They Told 88
Let's Take a Trip 89

Art

Patchwork Quilt 90
Squiggles. 91
Squiggles (reproducible) 92
A Is for Artist 93
Place and Trace Patterns 94
Place and Trace Patterns (reproducible) 95
Shiny Shape Mobiles. 96

INTRODUCTION

When children work or play together in pairs or groups using basic social skills in order to achieve any common goal, they are cooperating. *Cooperative learning* simply means that children work together, applying social skills in order to achieve an academic goal. For example, in a primary-level cooperative learning classroom, you might see pairs of children reading the same story, then taking turns retelling the story to each other to compare how each of them feels about the characters and plot. As one child speaks, the other is listening, showing interest in his or her partner's ideas. Or you might see a group of three students measuring objects in the classroom, with one using a ruler, another writing down the measurements on a graph or chart, while a third is encouraging the group, checking for accuracy, or making positive suggestions.

Like the members of a team, the members of a cooperative learning group are discovering how to share responsibility and how each member can contribute something special and important.

Why Cooperative Learning?

In a classroom where students rarely work cooperatively, energy that could be spent on learning and discovery is expended in competing for grades or vying to command more of the teacher's attention. Moreover, students may be missing two important aspects of their education—learning to work independently of an adult and learning to work effectively with peers. In a cooperative learning environment, on the other hand, students are encouraged to interact with one another, pooling their critical thinking skills to solve problems with decreased dependence on the teacher. In addition, in a competitive atmosphere the self esteem of "underachievers" is often undermined and their lack of motivation perpetuated. In a cooperative learning classroom all children are motivated by their sense of responsibility to their groups. They experience enhanced self esteem along with increased trust in others. Perhaps most importantly, students develop a sense of camaraderie and learn an important life lesson: no task is too big if we work together.

How Cooperative Learning Works

Setting up a cooperative learning environment in your classroom is really quite simple. Here are the basics:

- Students work in pairs or small groups, guided by the teacher.
- Each group member plays one or more specific roles in completing the work.
- Each group member is responsible for learning all the material.
- Group members are encouraged to communicate, share, and help one another.
- The teacher acts as facilitator, setting objectives, suggesting ways to divide tasks, monitoring behavior, and giving support, encouragement, and recognition.
- The group's progress is evaluated by the group members themselves as well as by the teacher. Criteria for evaluation include individual performance as well as the performance of the group as a whole.

This book is designed to help you get cooperative learning started in your classroom and to provide you with lots of fun and fascinating activities for your students to do together.

How This Book Is Organized

The book is divided into three sections:

A Cooperative Learning Classroom
Primary Activities (Grades K-3)
Intermediate Activities (Grades 4-6)

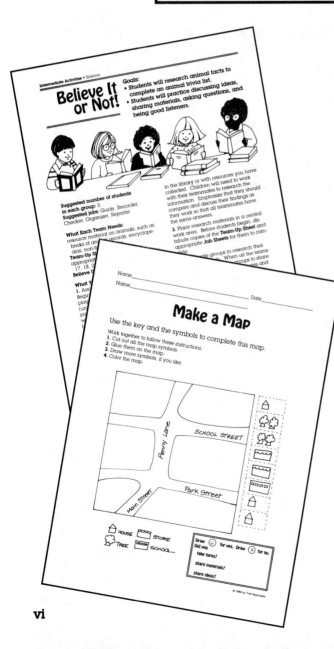

The **Cooperative Learning Classroom** section includes:

- ideas for introducing the meaning of cooperation and teamwork to your students
- suggestions for assigning teams and tasks
- aids for keeping track of and evaluating progress
- additional helpful hints
- bulletin board patterns
- reproducible pages
- an introductory activity on cooperative learning for primary students and one for intermediate students

The **Primary Activities (K-3)** section includes:

- simple activities across the curriculum for teams of two (reading/language arts, science, math, social studies, art)
- student reproducible pages

The **Intermediate Activities (4-6)** section includes:

- activities across the curriculum for teams of three or more (reading/language arts, science, math, social studies, art)
- student reproducible pages

Introducing Cooperative Learning

Introduce the idea of cooperative learning to your students by talking about teamwork. How does a Little League baseball team or soccer team play together? Get the "ball rolling" by asking questions such as the following:

- Does everyone on the team do the same job?
- How is it decided who will be the pitcher on a baseball team?...who will be the catcher?... who will play different positions in the field?
- What would happen if half the players didn't show up?
- What would happen if some didn't try their hardest?
- What would happen if the team members couldn't get along?
- What are the qualities of a "good sport" or a good team player?

A COOPERATIVE LEARNING CLASSROOM

Then go on to talk about how teamwork helps people in other areas besides sports. How do children team up to complete jobs like cleaning up a room, giving a bath to a dog, clearing the table after a meal, and so on? Is it easier if one person does the job alone or if two or more people work together? Does everyone do the same thing, or is it better if different people do different parts of the job?

Finally, ask students if they think teamwork can work in school. Raise questions such as these:

- Do you think you could work on a math assignment, write a story or report, or read a story with a partner or a group?
- Which activities would you like to do with a partner or a group? Are there some activities you would rather do alone?
- What are the advantages and disadvantages of working with a partner or a group?

Explain that another word for teamwork or working together in school is *cooperative learning.* Announce that the students will do an activity that will give them some idea about how to be a good cooperative learning partner (primary) or group member (intermediate).

Working Together: Primary

Primary-grade students work best in partner-pairs rather than in larger groups. For some activities, you might want to assign specific tasks to each partner. For others, invite children to decide for themselves how the jobs might be divided. Rotate partners often so that different children will get used to working together. Also, make sure that everyone gets a chance to practice roles that require leadership. Having children fill out the the **Partners' Team-Up Sheet** (page 11) will help you monitor how students have divided their assignments.

Try the following introductory activity to guide children in deciding how they might divide the tasks involved.

Can You Find Us?

Materials: **Partners All!** bulletin board pattern (page 9), 3" x 5" index cards, slips of paper, a bag, **Can You Find Us?** puzzle (page 10), **Partners' Team-Up Sheet** (page 11)

Create a permanent **Partners All!** bulletin board. In advance, prepare enough "partners" patterns for the class. Display the patterns on a bulletin board titled **Partners All!** Then label each index card with a student's name.

Explain that you are going to give the class an assignment to complete in partner-pairs. To help children pair up, write numbers on slips of paper so that each number appears on two slips. Then have children pick the slips out of a grab bag. The students with matching numbers are partners. Post the partners' names together on the **Partners All!** bulletin board. (For subsequent activities, you might want to pair off students by abilities, interests, readers with non-readers, etc.)

Then announce to the class that each pair of partners will get a puzzle to figure out, and hand out one **Can You Find Us?** puzzle to each pair. Tell the children to look at their puzzles, but not to start them yet. First, invite children to share ideas for how the partners will divide the work. You might help by suggesting that they could each be responsible for finding three people or animals, or they could take turns reading the questions and finding the pictures. Then give one **Partners' Team-Up Sheet** to each pair and help children fill in what their jobs will be. (Children who haven't learned to write yet can draw pictures.) Give the children about ten minutes to complete their **Can You Find Us?** puzzles.

After the children have finished their puzzles, talk briefly about how to work well with a partner. With the class, develop the following list of social skills:

Ways to Act with a Partner

- we speak quietly together
- we take turns
- we share materials
- we share ideas
- we are good listeners
- we speak kindly and politely

Write the list on a large sheet of paper, and post it in the room.

Partners All!

Bulletin Board Patterns

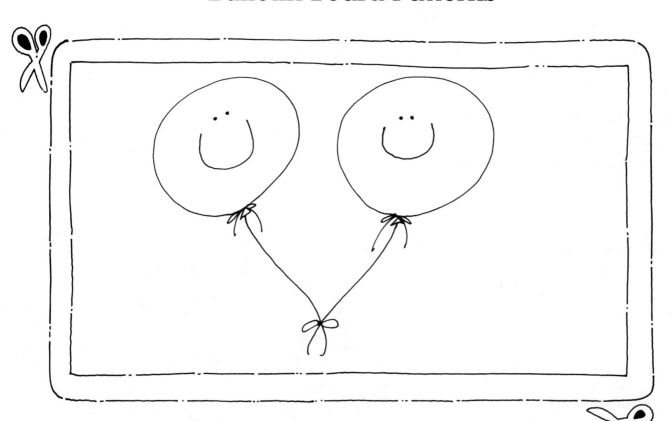

How to create a permanent **Partners All!** bulletin board:

Dan   Jen   Yuki   Lee   Cindy   Rob   Lisa   Ben

Pauline   Josh   Adam   Kim   Rosa   Dawn   Noel   Joey

Name_____Date_____

Name_____

Can You Find Us?

Work together to follow these instructions:

1. Draw a circle around a girl with a ponytail.
2. Draw a square around a dog with spots.
3. Draw a triangle around a boy on a swing.
4. Draw a line under a girl on a seesaw.
5. Draw a wiggly line under a squirrel in a tree.
6. Draw an arrow pointing to a cat.

Partners' Team-Up Sheet

Fill in this sheet with your partner. Draw a picture or write about what you will do.

Name _____   Name _____

Date _____   Date _____

I will   **I will**

_____   _____

_____   _____

_____   _____

_____   _____

_____   _____

Working Together: Intermediate

Most intermediate-grade students have developed the organizational and social skills needed to work in groups of three or more, with each group member assuming a specific role: that of Guide, Recorder, Checker, Booster, Organizer, or Reporter, depending on the demands of the activity and the number of children in the group. The specific jobs of each group member are listed on the reproducible job sheets on pages 16 - 21.

For some activities, you might invite the group members to choose their own roles; for others, you might assign roles. Roles may be geared to individual students' abilities, so that everyone has a chance to perform confidently and successfully. On the other hand, you might want to encourage students to try out roles that will help them develop new strengths. A shy student, for example, might benefit from trying out a role that will give her or him a feeling for leadership. To be sure that each child has a chance to contribute in a variety of ways, change groups for each new project and see that roles are rotated. Some ongoing activities may even lend themselves to daily role rotation within the project.

For the following introductory activity, let the students choose their own roles, helping them get organized if necessary.

Prefix Pursuit

Materials: Terrific Teammates! bulletin board pattern (page 14), scissors, index cards, dictionaries, **Team-Up Sheet** (page 15), **Job Sheets** (pages 16 - 21)

Prepare a **Terrific Teammates!** bulletin board. In advance, copy and cut out six copies of the **Terrific Teammates!** tiger pattern. Label each with one of the following roles: Guide, Recorder, Checker, Booster, Organizer, Reporter. Display the tigers on a bulletin board titled **Terrific Teammates!**

Explain to the students that they are going to have an assignment to do, but they won't be working individually—they'll be working in teams of six, and each team member will have his or her special job to do. Tell students they'll be allowed to talk quietly, share ideas, and help each other. That's what teamwork is all about. (If the class doesn't divide evenly, work out how to give one or two students two jobs, or two students might share a job.)

Now explain the assignment. (You may want to vary or adapt the assignment according to the level of your class.) Each team will get a dictionary and a card with a prefix written on it. The challenge is to find twelve words that begin with that prefix, to figure out the meaning of the prefix, and to learn the meaning of each word. (Suggested prefixes: *pre-, re-, un-, mis-, pro-*)

Before students begin, direct their attention to the **Terrific Teammates!** bulletin board. What do they think each tiger's job might be in completing the prefix assignment?

- Which group member might explain the assignment to the others?
- Which member would write down the words?
- Which group member would make sure the words are spelled correctly?
- Which member might help everyone get along together?
- Which member would figure out what to do first?
- Which member would report back to the class the results of the team's work?

Next, divide the class into groups, giving each group a copy of the **Team-Up Sheet** and one copy of each **Job Sheet**. Discuss with the class the specific jobs listed on each sheet. Then guide the groups by helping students choose jobs and showing how to fill out the job sheets. (The Recorder, Checker, and Reporter will have to wait until the assignment is completed to finish their job sheets.) The group Recorder might fill out the **Team-Up Sheet**. Note: Assure students that they won't always have the same jobs. Everyone will get turns having each job. In addition, make it clear that there won't always be six people on a team—often there will be three, four, or five.

Now the teams are ready for their prefix assignment. Remind them that this is *not* a test. Also, emphasize that they shouldn't worry or be discouraged if the group experiment doesn't work perfectly the first time. Assure them that things will go more smoothly as they get used to this way of working together. Then provide enough time for the assignment. When all groups are ready, ask the reporters to give their groups' results to the class.

Afterwards, help students conclude that, in addition to other important qualities for a good team player, a good cooperative learner needs to develop these cooperation skills:

Cooperation Skills
- taking turns
- sharing materials
- being a good listener
- sharing ideas and feelings
- asking questions
- speaking kindly and politely to others
- speaking quietly
- giving compliments
- staying on task

List the cooperation skills and prominently display them in the room. As children become more accustomed to a cooperative learning environment, these skills will become more and more meaningful, and their importance will become increasingly apparent.

Terrific Teammates!

Bulletin Board Pattern

Team-Up Sheet

Complete this sheet with your team. Write the name of each team member and the job each member will have.

Teammates   **Jobs**

_____   _____

_____   _____

_____   _____

_____   _____

_____   _____

Name_____ Date_____

Guide's Job Sheet

Jobs   **The People in My Group**

Guide   _____
Recorder   _____
Checker   _____
Booster   _____
Organizer   _____
Reporter   _____

✔ **My job is to:**

_____ Understand my group's assignment.
_____ Get the group together.
_____ Explain the assignment to the group.
_____ Make sure everyone shares and takes turns.
_____ Help to work out problems.
_____ Make sure our group finishes on time.

Our assignment is

_____

_____

_____

_____

_____

Recorder's Job Sheet

Jobs

Guide
Recorder
Checker
Booster
Organizer
Reporter

The People in My Group

_____
_____
_____
_____
_____
_____

✔ **My job is to:**
_____ Write down what my group learned.
_____ Write down how my group worked together.
_____ Write down problems we had and how we could
       solve them next time.

How My Group Worked Together:

	✔ often	✔ sometimes	✔ not often
We took turns.	_____	_____	_____
We shared materials.	_____	_____	_____
We listened to each other.	_____	_____	_____
We shared ideas.	_____	_____	_____
We asked questions.	_____	_____	_____
We spoke kindly to each other.	_____	_____	_____
We spoke quietly.	_____	_____	_____
We gave compliments.	_____	_____	_____
We stayed on task.	_____	_____	_____

Name_____ Date_____

Checker's Job Sheet

Jobs

Guide
Recorder
Checker
Booster
Organizer
Reporter

The People in My Group

_____
_____
_____
_____
_____
_____

✔ **My job is to:**

____ Make sure everyone is here.
____ Make sure we have the materials we need.
____ Make sure everyone is doing his or her job.
____ Make sure everyone's work is correct.

Materials Check List

What We Need

✔
What We Have

_____

_____

_____

_____

_____

_____

Name_____ Date_____

Booster's Job Sheet

Jobs

Guide
Recorder
Checker
Booster
Organizer
Reporter

The People in My Group

_____

_____

_____

_____

_____

✔ My job is to:

____ Encourage the people in my group.
____ Remind group members to give compliments.
____ Help solve disagreements.
____ Remind people to speak kindly to each other.

Words of Encouragement

_____

_____

_____

_____

_____

_____

_____

_____

Name_____ Date_____

Organizer's Job Sheet

Jobs   **The People in My Group**

Guide   _____
Recorder   _____
Checker   _____
Booster   _____
Organizer   _____
Reporter   _____

✔ **My job is to:**

—— Help decide which materials my group will need.
—— Help my group decide the steps we need to take to
       do our assignment.
—— Help my group figure out the best order of steps.
—— Help the members of my group share the information
       they have learned.
—— Lead group discussions.

What My Group Needs to Do:

1. _____

2. _____

3. _____

4. _____

5. _____

Reporter's Job Sheet

Jobs   **The People in My Group**

Guide   _____

Recorder   _____

Checker   _____

Booster   _____

Organizer   _____

Reporter   _____

✔ **My job is to:**

____ Get information from the Recorder about what my group has learned.

____ Go over with the group my report about what we have learned.

____ Give a report to the class about what my group has learned.

What My Group Learned:

_____

_____

_____

_____

_____

_____

How Did It Go?

After completing the introductory activity (**Can You Find Us?** for primary; **Prefix Pursuit** for intermediate), meet with the class as a whole to evaluate their results. (With **intermediate** students, first ask the guides and checkers to report on how cooperation worked in their groups. Then open the discussion to the class as a whole.) Did the partners or teams run into any problems working together? How could they have been solved by practicing better cooperation skills?

You might have a group role-play the scene that led up to a particular problem, then "freeze" when the problem arises. Ask the class to suggest ways in which the group could have prevented or handled the problem. Then have the group "replay" the scene in a more constructive way. You might also have group members change roles and act out the scene again.

Keeping Track

To help you keep track of each group member's progress with regard to one or more social skills, use the reproducible pages **Keeping Track: Primary** (page 24), and **Keeping Track: Intermediate** (page 25). Reproduce and keep them on record to monitor students' progress.

Helpful Hints

- As you and your students sample the activities in this book, you will find suggestions for using the reproducible materials in this section. Keep these pages in a folder for easy access. Feel free to adapt or extend their use to suit your group's needs.

- Note that **Keeping Track** reproducible pages may be used for every activity to monitor the specific social and cooperative skill you wish to stress.

- Prepare materials in advance.

- Try to establish groups with children of different abilities. Emphasize that it is important for every member of the group to learn or do what is expected.

- Help children create jobs as they become necessary for completing an activity. Not every role will be needed for each activity, and for some, one child may be responsible for more than one role.

- Introduce activities to all members of a group. Make sure everyone understands the assignment before the group begins.

- Encourage students to use their problem-solving skills and to seek help from each other before asking you for assistance.

- Reward individuals and groups for working cooperatively. (See **Just Rewards**, page 26; **Perfect Partners Award**, page 27; **Terrific Team Award**, page 28.)

- Be available to help the students when they need you.

And...most of all, enjoy watching your students cooperate and learn!

Keeping Track (Primary)

Choose a social skill to encourage for this particular activity. Make a check or tally mark next to each partner's name when you see the child practicing the skill.

Date(s) _____

Skill to Practice _____

Partners _____ Partners _____

_____ _____

Partners _____ Partners _____

_____ _____

Partners _____ Partners _____

_____ _____

Partners _____ Partners _____

_____ _____

Partners _____ Partners _____

_____ _____

Partners _____ Partners _____

_____ _____

Partners _____ Partners _____

_____ _____

Keeping Track (Intermediate)

Choose a social skill to encourage for this particular activity.
Then make a check or tally mark next to each group member's
name when you see the student practicing the skill.

Date(s) _____

Skill to Practice _____

Team:

_____   _____

_____   _____

_____   _____

Team:

_____   _____

_____   _____

_____   _____

Team:

_____   _____

_____   _____

_____   _____

Team:

_____   _____

_____   _____

_____   _____

Just Rewards

Terrific Teammate!

Sensational Problem Solver!

Super Listener!

Perfect Partners Award

Date: _____

This award is given to partners

_____   _____
Name   Name

for their great work.

They _____

_____

_____

_____

_____
Teacher's Signature

Terrific Team Award

SUPER

Date: _____

This award is given to teammates

_____   _____

_____   _____

_____   _____

for their excellent cooperation.

They _____

_____

_____
Teacher's Signature

Create a Treat

Goals:
- **Children will follow directions to create peanut butter treats.**
- **Children will learn to share tasks and responsibilities.**

What Each Pair Needs:
peanut butter
rice crackers
raisins
plastic knives
paper plates
napkins
Partners' Team-Up Sheet (page 11)

What You Do:
1. Assign students to partner-pairs. Then introduce the activity by talking about the children's favorite foods. Ask, "Who likes peanut butter?" "Who likes raisins?" "Who likes crackers?" Ask the partners to talk about ways these three ingredients could be put together to make a delicious treat.

2. Show children how to spread the peanut butter on the rice crackers, encouraging them to use the raisins to create faces or other designs.

3. Write the following instructions on the chalkboard and read them aloud.
- Spread the peanut butter on the cracker.
- Use the raisins to make a design.

4. Discuss why it is important for children to follow instructions.

5. Now place materials where children can share them. Ask partners to think about what jobs might be shared in making the treats.
- One person spreads the peanut butter while the other child decorates with raisins.
- Both children spread the peanut butter and take turns decorating.
- One child holds the cracker while the other spreads the peanut butter and decorates.

6. Give one copy of the **Partners' Team-Up Sheet** to each pair and help children fill it in.

7. Encourage partner-pairs to try as many different designs and faces as time permits.

8. Allow time for pairs to show their favorite designs to their classmates. Then invite the children to enjoy their treats for a snack.

Focus on Cooperation Suggest that students talk about how well they worked together. Did any problems arise? How were they solved? How might children work together better next time?

Come Share a Book!

Goals:
▪ **Children will build reading motivation by creating a poster for the school or class library.**
▪ **Children will practice sharing materials and ideas.**

What Each Pair Needs:
poster paper
crayons/markers
Partners' Team-Up Sheet (page 11)

What You Do:
1. Introduce the activity by helping children recall visits to the library. Ask such guiding questions as:
▪ Which library have you visited lately? The public library? The school's? The classroom's?
▪ Were there any colorful posters hanging in the library when you visited?
▪ Why might the librarian put up a poster in a library? What would a library poster tell about?

2. Display a sheet of blank poster paper and print in large letters across the top, "Visit the Library—Come Share a Book!" Encourage partner-pairs to discuss possi-

ble illustrations to draw on the poster that would make children want to visit the library. Their picture ideas may include book covers, characters from favorite stories, bookshelves, happy children sharing books, a parent and child reading together.

3. Now invite children to work with partners to make a library poster using your title or one of their own. Pair students and place materials where children can share them.

4. Ask children to discuss how they might share the work before they begin.
▪ One person writes the words and the other draws the pictures.
▪ Both children draw the pictures and then take turns writing the words.
▪ One person outlines or sketches the pictures and words and the other fills in the colors and details.

5. Give one **Partners' Team-Up Sheet** to each pair and assist as partners fill it in.

6. Allow time for partner-pairs to complete their posters and present them to the class.

Focus on Cooperation Talk with the class about sharing materials and ideas. Were there any problems? How could they be avoided or dealt with next time? If a partner-pair experienced sharing problems, you might have them act out what happened. Then ask the class to discuss how the problem might have been solved or avoided.

Mystery Rhyme Time

Goals:
- **Children will apply their knowledge of nursery rhymes to reading picture clues.**
- **Children will practice listening and sharing ideas.**

What Each Pair Needs:
nursery rhyme anthologies
drawing paper pre-folded in fourths
crayons/markers
Partners' Team-Up Sheet (page 11)

What You Do:
1. Draw each of the following simple pictures in one quadrant of the drawing paper: a little girl, a lamb, a school, children at school. These will be the picture clues for the nursery rhyme "Mary Had a Little Lamb."

2. Invite children to name and recite familiar nursery rhymes. Then show children the picture clues and challenge them to guess which nursery rhyme the picture clues illustrate.

3. Explain to children that they will work with partners to think of and draw picture clues for other nursery rhymes that will be used for a mystery-rhyme guessing game.

4. Pair students and place materials in a central work area. Ask partner-pairs to confer about the jobs needed to complete the activity. On the chalkboard, list their ideas, including:
- finding and reading nursery rhymes
- deciding on clues
- drawing clues
- coloring clues
- presenting clues

Ask partners to decide what they will do first. Then help partner-pairs fill out a **Partners' Team-Up Sheet.**

5. Allow time for partners to draw their four picture clues. Then have pairs trade clues and guess each other's mystery rhymes. After, encourage children to recite the rhymes in chorus.

Focus on Cooperation Discuss with the class how well they listened and shared ideas with their partners. Why are these skills important when working together?

What Could It Be?

Goals:
- Children will use verbal clues and their imaginations to identify items in a box.
- Children will practice sharing ideas and being good listeners.

What You Need:
gift-wrapped box (or drawing of one)
surprise item of your choice

What Each Pair Needs:
crayons/markers
Partners' Team-Up Sheet (page 11)
What Could It Be? reproducible
  (page 33)

What You Do:
1. Introduce the activity by displaying a gift-wrapped box with a surprise inside. Challenge the students to guess the surprise. Then give students several clues, including "It is smaller than a ____, but bigger than a ____."

2. Let students work with partners, and arrange materials for children to share. Pass out one **What Could It Be?** reproducible page to each pair.

3. Explain that this activity has two parts:
- First, partners will brainstorm and write down a list of ten things they think might be in the box. (Younger students may draw pictures.)
- Next, they will choose one of their guesses to draw inside the surprise box on the **What Could It Be?** reproducible page.

4. Ask partners to plan how they will share the work involved before they begin.
- One person thinks of ideas and the other one draws the pictures.
- Both children think of ideas and take turns drawing pictures.
- Both children think of ideas, then one draws pictures while the other labels them.

5. After children have completed **What Could It Be?** encourage them to compare their answers with classmates'. Finally, show children what really is inside the box. How many partner-pairs guessed correctly?

Focus on Cooperation Talk about how sharing ideas and being a good listener go together. Have students report on the ideas they gave to and received from their partners.

Name_____ Date_____

Name_____

What Could It Be?

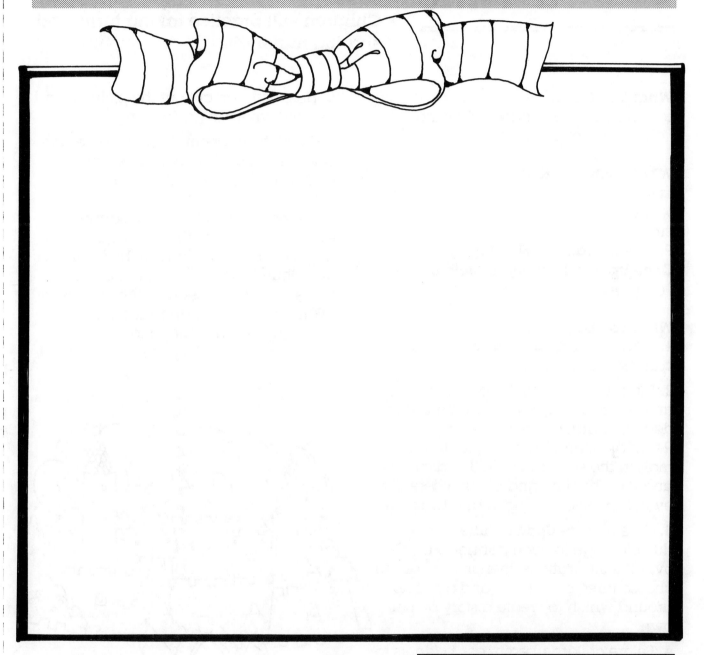

What do you think is inside the box? Work together to come up with ideas. Then draw a picture to show what you think is inside the surprise box.

Draw 😃 for yes. Draw 🙁 for no.
Did you

speak quietly?

share ideas?

listen to each other?

Once Upon a Time

Goals:
- **Children will choose characters and a setting to come up with their own story scene.**
- **Children will practice taking turns and sharing materials.**

What You Need:
a picture-book illustration showing characters and setting

What Each Pair Needs:
scissors
white glue
crayons
Partners' Team-Up Sheet (page 11)
Once Upon a Time reproducible (page 35)

What You Do:
1. Arrange partner-pairs where they can share materials.

2. Introduce the activity by displaying an illustration from a picture book that depicts characters and a setting. Remind children that people and animals in the story are called characters and that the time and place where the events in a story happen are the setting.

3. Give a **Once Upon a Time** reproducible page to each partner-pair. Go over the illustrations, then invite pairs to choose three characters and a setting around which to create a story of their own.

4. Before children begin, ask partners to talk about ways to complete the activity together.
- One child chooses the setting, the other chooses the characters.
- One child cuts, and the other child pastes.
- One child cuts and pastes, and the other child colors.

5. Help children cut out the pictures and explain where to paste them.

6. Allow time for children to create and color their **Once Upon a Time** scenes and share them with the class.

Focus on Cooperation Ask partners to evaluate how well they took turns and shared. They can indicate by "thumbs up," "thumbs down," or "thumbs sideways." Then discuss with the class why taking turns and sharing materials is important when working together.

Once Upon a Time

Work together to make your own **Once Upon a Time** story scene.

Directions:
1. Cut out all the pictures.
2. Choose three characters.
3. Paste the pictures in the space to make your story scene.
4. Color your scene.

Does Your Boat Float?

Goals:
- **Children will experiment to find out which objects float and use them to create unusual "boats."**
- **Children will practice sharing materials and ideas.**

What You Need:
a tank or pan of water

What Each Pair Needs:
a variety of objects for creating boats
   (paper clips, pencils, corks, straws,
   metal spoons, wooden blocks, cut-up
   kitchen sponges, pieces of Styrofoam,
   empty 1/2 pint milk cartons, pipe
   cleaners, yarn, and so on)
string
scissors
Partners' Team-Up Sheet (page 11)
Does Your Boat Float?
   reproducible (page 37)

What You Do:
1. Display a tank or pan of water and objects for testing. Introduce the activity by asking volunteers to predict which objects they think will float. Record students' predictions on the chalkboard or on **Does Your Boat Float?** reproducible page. Then tell children they will have a chance to experiment to find out which objects float.

2. Give one copy of the **Does Your Boat Float?** reproducible page to each partner-pair. Read aloud the directions and explain how to fill in the three-part chart. Point out that children will draw the object, make a prediction before they test it, and write what happens after they test it.

3. Call attention to the challenge at the bottom of the page, asking children to use the objects that float to make a "boat." Assure children that their "boat" can be unusual and need not resemble a real boat. Suggest that children might use string to attach objects together.

4. Place materials where they can be shared. Ask partners to discuss how the jobs could be divided.
- One partner tests the objects while the other completes the chart.
- Partners take turns testing objects and completing the chart.
- Both partners brainstorm ideas for the "boat" and create it together.

5. When the "boats" are completed, have the partner-pairs present them to the class, then "sail" them in the water.

Focus on Cooperation Discuss the importance of working together. What problems can arise if one partner refuses to work or does all the work? Do children think they would each learn evenly? Can students suggest any strategies for resolving these problems?

Name_____ Date_____

Name_____

Does Your Boat Float?

Which of these things will float? Try some of them and see! Fill in the chart as you experiment.

Draw it

Try it.

	Will it float? Guess **yes** or **no**.	Does it float? Write **yes** or **no**.
[ ]	_____	_____
[ ]	_____	_____
[ ]	_____	_____
[ ]	_____	_____

Challenge: Use the things that float to make a "boat." Then try it out. Does your "boat" float?
If you want to experiment more, use the back of this page.

Draw 😊 for yes. Draw 🙁 for no.
Did you

share materials?

share ideas?

listen to each other?

speak kindly?

© 1994 by Troll Associates.

Using Your Senses

Goals:
▪ **Children will use their five senses to explore objects.**
▪ **Children will practice speaking together quietly and taking turns.**

What You Need:
a brown bag filled with pretzel sticks

What Each Pair Needs:
paper plates
items for experimenting:
   lemon slices, sugar cubes, fabric
   swatches, rattles or pre-made shakers
   (rice in two paper cups taped together
   or in pint-size milk cartons)
crayons
Partners' Team-Up Sheet (page 11)
Using Your Senses reproducible
  (page 39)

What You Do:
1. Present children with a closed brown
bag filled with pretzel sticks. Challenge
them to guess what is in the bag by
concentrating on what they hear, smell,
touch, and taste. In turn, have volunteers try the following:
▪ Shake the bag and listen. What do
  they hear?
▪ Smell what's inside. What do they
  smell?
▪ Feel what's inside. What do they feel?
▪ Taste what's inside (with their eyes
  closed). What do they taste?

Finally, invite volunteers to look inside
to check their guesses.

2. Have the children share the pretzels
as you print the following words and
symbols on the chalkboard:

3. Review with the class the five senses
that help us learn about our world. Ask
volunteers to tell which sense or senses
were most helpful for discovering what
was in the bag. Lead children to conclude that sometimes we use only one
sense, but usually we use more than
one at a time.

4. Pair the children and give each pair
one or two copies of the **Using Your
Senses** reproducible page. Place the
materials to be tested in a central work
area. Then discuss how children could
take turns in this activity. Their suggestions should include testing the objects
and filling in the reproducible page.

5. Now invite partners to work together
to see, hear, taste, smell, and/or touch
each object. (Warn them which objects
are not to be tasted.) Instruct them to
work together to fill out the reproducible
page as they go along.

6. As they work, praise children who
are working cooperatively and taking
turns. When they have completed the
Using Your Senses reproducible page,
have children compare their findings
with other partner-pairs.

Focus on Cooperation Discuss with the
class why it is important for partners to
talk to each other during an activity.
Why is it important to talk in quiet voices? What if everyone spoke loudly?

Name_____ Date_____

Name_____

Using Your Senses

First, draw the object. Then write a ✔ next to each sense you use.

Draw it!

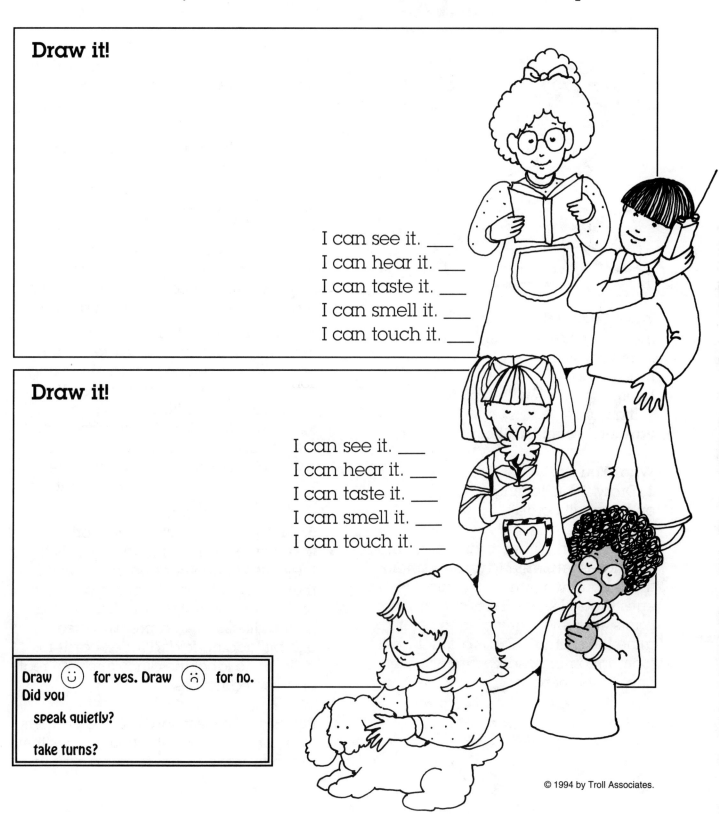

I can see it. ___
I can hear it. ___
I can taste it. ___
I can smell it. ___
I can touch it. ___

Draw it!

I can see it. ___
I can hear it. ___
I can taste it. ___
I can smell it. ___
I can touch it. ___

Draw ☺ for yes. Draw ☹ for no.
Did you

speak quietly?

take turns?

In a Prehistoric Zoo

Goals:
- **Children will learn about dinosaur characteristics by creating model dinosaurs.**
- **Children will practice sharing materials, expressing ideas, and being good listeners.**

What Each Pair Needs:
modeling clay in different colors
index cards
markers
reference books with pictures of
    dinosaurs
Partners' Team-Up Sheet (page 11)

What You Do:
1. Draw the following
on the chalkboard:

Can children tell what kind of animal
left these footprints? (a bird) Explain
that about two hundred years ago, scientists found several sets of giant footprints, for which they tried to determine the animal. Draw a giant fossil
footprint on the chalkboard like the
one shown here:

Continue explaining that giant bones
and teeth were also found. Ask if anyone can guess what kind of animal they
came from (a dinosaur).

2. Explain that scientists are still learning about dinosaurs and what they
may have looked like. Invite children
to imagine dinosaurs and create their
own models.

3. Group children in pairs. Arrange
materials where they can be shared,
including reference materials rich with
drawings and photographs of dinosaurs.

4. Ask partners to talk together about
the dinosaurs they wish to create and
which jobs might be shared in making
the models. Get the class started by
suggesting possibilities.
- Both children share ideas about what
  kinds of dinosaurs to make.
- One child shapes the clay into the
  body while the other creates limbs, a
  tail, and a head.

5. Allow time for children to work
together to create as many models as
they wish. Encourage them to experiment with different shapes, clay colors,
and surface textures. Display the completed dinosaurs in a prehistoric zoo
exhibit, adding folded index cards for
children to label the dinosaurs with real
or invented names.

Focus on Cooperation Ask the partners
to report on and evaluate the ways they
found to share the tasks in this activity.

Starry, Starry Night

Goals:
- **Children will learn about constellations by creating and naming constellations of their own.**
- **Children will practice speaking quietly, sharing materials, and conferring about ideas.**

What You Need:
a ladle

What Each Pair Needs:
gummed gold or silver stars
two sheets of black construction paper
chalk
Partners' Team-Up Sheet (page 11)

What You Do:
1. Introduce the activity by asking, "What would you see if you looked up at the nighttime sky?" (moon, stars)
2. Draw the following picture of the Big Dipper constellation on the chalkboard:

Explain that a star pattern like this can sometimes be seen at night. People long ago gave these star patterns names that we still use today. Such patterns are called constellations. Inform children that this constellation is called the Big Dipper. Show children the ladle, pointing out how the shape resembles that of the star pattern.

3. Tell children that they will create their own constellations. Demonstrate by asking volunteers to place gummed stars on black construction paper in random order. Then ask another volunteer to draw a line from star to star with chalk to create a picture or design. Ask the children to study the design and suggest names for the imaginary constellation.

4. Provide each child in a pair with his or her own set of star stickers and black construction paper. Give partners time to discuss how they will share the task.
- Place stars on the page.
- Trade papers with your partner.
- Connect the stars to form a pattern.
- Name your partner's constellation.
Alternately, partners could make each constellation together.

5. Give one **Partners' Team-Up Sheet** to each pair and help children fill it out.

6. Now invite the pairs to create their own constellations. Display their completed work on a bulletin board titled "Starry, Starry Night."

Focus on Cooperation Ask the partner-pairs to share with the class how they divided the tasks in this activity. Did partner-pairs work on different aspects of the project? Was there a cooperative technique that children would like to try next time?

At the Toy Shop

Goals:
- Children will count sets of toys in order to create a table or chart.
- Children will practice sharing ideas, being attentive listeners, speaking politely, and comparing answers.

What You Need:
several blocks or sets of common toys

What Each Pair Needs:
crayons/markers
Partners' Team-Up Sheet (page 11)
At the Toy Shop reproducibles (page 43)

What You Do:

1. Display several blocks, or any other set of like toys. Recall with children that the same types of toys are usually displayed together at a toy shop. What other toys might children find at a toy shop?

2. Group children in pairs and give each child a copy of the **At the Toy Shop** reproducible page. Place crayons and markers where they can be shared.

3. Have children focus their attention on the toy shop pictured on the top half of the page. Explain that because the shop is such a mess, the owner doesn't know the number of toys. Tell the children that they can help by coloring and counting each set of toys for the shop-keeper.

4. Point out the table at the bottom of the page. Explain that a table is a type of chart that organizes information in a clear and easy-to-read way. Show students where to write the number of toys in each set.

5. Ask partners to complete their papers and compare their answers. If their answers do not agree, have partners work together to find the mistakes and correct them.

6. Challenge students with the activity at the bottom of the page. Read the challenge aloud. Point out that using the numbers from the table may help find the answer quickly.

Focus on Cooperation Talk about why it is important for partners to speak kindly and politely to each other. What if you disagree with your partner or think she or he is making a mistake?

Name_____ Date_____

At the Toy Shop

Find all the different sets of toys and then count them.

Color the balls red. Color the cars blue. Color the teddy bears brown.
Color the sailboats green.

Count the toys in each set. Fill in the table below.

Toys at the Shop

Kinds of Toys	How Many?
	_____
	_____
	_____
	_____

Challenge: How many toys in all are in the shop?_____

Inch by Inch

Goals:
- **Children will measure classroom objects using a six-inch ruler.**
- **Children will practice sharing materials and ideas.**

What Each Pair Needs:
six-inch ruler (or six-inch lengths
  of string)
drawing paper pre-folded into thirds
crayons
Partners' Team-Up Sheet (page 11)

What You Do:
1. Display several six-inch rulers, asking children to tell what they are and how they are used. Explain that these rulers measure only up to 6 inches. Enlist a volunteer to use the ruler to measure a book. Then ask: "Is the book 6 inches long? Is it less than 6 inches long? Is it more than 6 inches?"

2. Divide the class into partner-pairs and give one ruler and a sheet of drawing paper to each. Help students label each section of the paper as follows:

6"   more   less

3. Tell children that they will work with their partners to measure as many different objects in the room as time allows. Explain that after they measure each object, they will draw a picture of it

under the correct heading on the chart. For example, if a partner measures a pen that is 3 inches long, he or she should draw a picture of the pen in the column labeled "less" because 3 inches is "less" than 6 inches.

4. Give the partner-pairs time to decide together how they will share the work involved before they begin.
- One child holds an object while the other measures.
- One child measures while the other fills in the chart.
- Children take turns measuring and filling in the chart.

5. Distribute **Partners' Team-Up Sheets,** and help pairs fill them in.

6. Allow time for children to measure and complete their charts. Then have partner-pairs gather and compare their findings.

Focus on Cooperation Ask the partner-pairs to compare the ways they found to share the tasks in this activity. Which task did they enjoy most and least?

Yours and Mine

Goals:
▪ **Children will divide different shapes into equal halves and use them to make designs.**
▪ **Children will practice speaking quietly, sharing materials, and exchanging ideas.**

What Each Pair Needs:
scissors
paper shapes such as circles, squares, rectangles, ovals, and triangles, all about 5 inches in diameter
glue or tape
12" x 18" construction paper
Partners' Team-Up Sheet (page 11)

What You Do:
1. Introduce the activity by calling two children to the front of the room and holding up a paper circle. Present the class with this problem: These two children have only one circle to share. How can they share the circle so that both children receive equal parts? When the suggestion is made to cut the circle in half, demonstrate how to carefully fold the circle in half and cut along the fold. Then give one part to each child, and ask how much of the circle each child has (half). Write the fraction "1/2" on the chalkboard.

2. Assign students to partners and place scissors and paper shapes where they can be shared. Invite children to work together to share each shape equally.

3. Ask children to discuss with their partners how they might divide the work before they begin.
▪ One partner folds while the other cuts.
▪ Both partners take turns cutting and folding.

4. Hand out one **Partners' Team-Up Sheet** to each pair and assist as children fill it in.

5. After an appropriate amount of time, ask children to count their shapes to make sure each partner has half of each. Then distribute large sheets of construction paper and invite each partner to create his or her own design with the shapes. Challenge children to make the designs different from their partners'. When children are satisfied with their designs, instruct them to glue the shapes on the paper.

Focus on Cooperation Discuss with the children that although partners had the same shapes, they came up with different designs. How does this demonstrate the importance of sharing ideas? (We can learn new ideas from other people.)

Picture This!

Goals:
- **Children will use geometric shapes to form a design.**
- **Children will help each other hone their visual discrimination skills.**

What Each Pair Needs:
scissors
glue
drawing paper
crayons
Partners' Team-Up Sheet (page 11)
Picture This! reproducible (page 47)

What You Do:
1. To introduce the activity, draw the following on the chalkboard:

2. Ask children to name the shapes they see. Explain that sometimes we can find different shapes in one object. To demonstrate, play a game of "I Spy." Ask children to look around the room for things made up of more than one shape.

3. Pair students and arrange materials in a central work space. Give a copy of the **Picture This!** reproducible page to each partner-pair. Challenge partners to identify the shapes used to create the house. Then explain that the shapes they need to make this picture are on the page. Explain that partners will need to cut out the shapes and paste them on drawing paper, but three of the shapes on the page will not be needed.

4. Ask partners to talk about how to divide up this task. List their suggestions on the chalkboard. Possibilities might include:
- cutting out shapes
- deciding which shapes are needed
- gluing shapes onto the page
- coloring the picture
Ask partners to decide which job they need to do first.

5. Have children complete their houses.

Focus on Cooperation Ask partner-pairs if they took turns doing any particular job during this activity. Which job was it? Why is taking turns important when working together?

Picture This!

Can you make this house? What shapes will you need? Work together to follow these instructions:

1. Cut out all the shapes.
2. Choose the shapes you need to make the picture.
3. Glue the shapes together on a sheet of paper.
4. Color the picture.

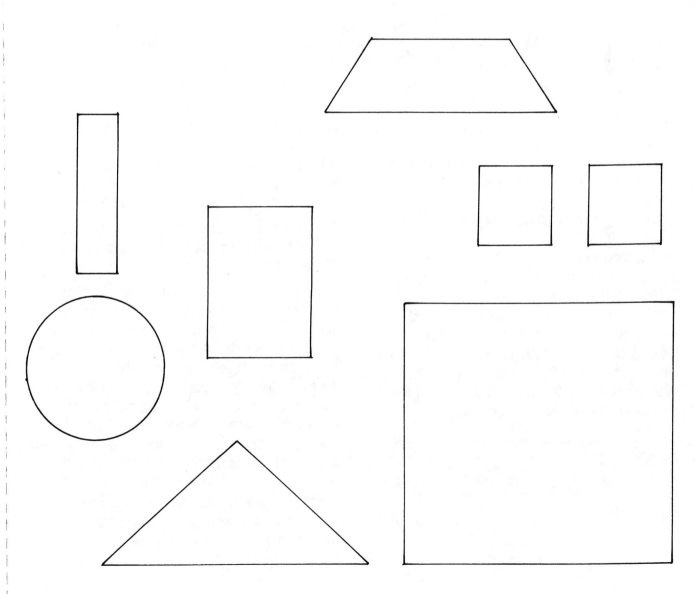

Pattern a Pattern

Goals:
- **Children will use colored beads to practice making patterns.**
- **Children will help each other enhance visual discrimination.**

What Each Pair Needs:
4 index cards
wooden beads of three different colors
markers (same colors as beads)
shoelaces
Partners' Team-Up Sheet (page 11)

What You Do:
1. Prepare in advance an index card with a pattern of circles in three different colors. Display the pattern card and call on a volunteer to copy the color pattern by stringing colored beads on a shoelace. Tell children that they will work with partners to create different bead patterns of their own.

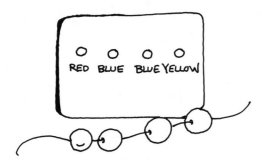

2. List these steps for the activity on the chalkboard.
- Draw patterns on index cards.
- Trade cards with partners.
- String beads to make the patterns.

3. Pair children and provide them with index cards, markers, beads, and shoelaces.

4. Instruct partners to draw and color two patterns each. Tell them to trade cards and copy each others' patterns by stringing beads. Afterwards, encourage partners to check each others' work. Suggest that one call off each color on the card while the other answers with the color of the corresponding bead. If there are any discrepancies, let partners correct them together.

Focus on Cooperation Evaluate with the class how well partner-pairs were able to speak softly. Did the class work quietly and cooperatively? Why is this important?

Where Am I?

Goals:
- Children will compare and contrast characteristics of different places by creating friezes.
- Children will practice sharing materials and ideas.

What You Need:
8 1/2" x 11" drawing paper
drawing pens or markers
tape

What Each Pair Needs:
8 1/2" x 11" drawing paper
crayons/markers
tape
Partners' Team-Up Sheet (page 11)

What You Do:
1. In advance, draw books on a sheet of drawing paper. On a second sheet draw bookshelves. On a third, a librarian. And on a fourth, a library card.

2. Choose four volunteers to each pick a sheet and describe the picture. Display the four clues in a row and challenge the children to answer the question, "If I see books, bookshelves, a librarian, and a library card, where am I?" (the library)

3. Ask four more children to help you tape the pictures in a row. Display the finished product and explain that a "frieze" is a series of drawings in a row. Invite children to create their own friezes of picture clues for other places in the school or neighborhood or a place they

have visited. Tell children that they will use the frieze later for a guessing game.

4. Give pairs of children four sheets of drawing paper and crayons or markers. Ask partners to discuss the jobs needed to complete the activity. List their ideas on the chalkboard. They may include:
- deciding on the special place
- brainstorming for clue ideas
- choosing and drawing four clues
- coloring clues

Ask partners to discuss where they should begin. Give one **Partners' Team-Up Sheet** to each pair, and help children complete it.

5. Instruct pairs to draw their four clues. When the clues are completed, have children tape their drawings in a row. Allow time for pairs to trade clues and guess each other's mystery places.

Focus on Cooperation Ask the partner-pairs how they decided which picture clues to draw. Were there any disagreements over the clues? Did some ideas have to be eliminated? Can the students suggest any strategies for resolving disagreements between partners?

Safety First!

Goals:
▪ **Children will learn the meanings of various safety signs and signals.**
▪ **Children will practice talking softly, taking turns, and sharing ideas.**

What You Need:
a 5″ red paper circle
a 5″ green paper circle

What Each Pair Needs:
crayons
Partners' Team-Up Sheet (page 11)
Safety First! reproducible (page 51)

What You Do:
1. Play a quick game of "Red Light, Green Light" with children running in place. Explain that when you hold up the "green light" (green circle), they may "go," and when you hold up a "red light" (red circle), they must "stop."

2. After the game, ask children to think about the red and green light signals they see in the street and ask how these signals help drivers and walkers. (They tell us when it's safe or unsafe to move.) Ask children to name other road signs they recall. Draw their ideas as they are named. For example:

Why are these signs important? (They help keep us safe.)

3. Assign students to partners and give each pair one copy of the **Safety First!** reproducible page. Discuss the meaning of each "no" sign at the top of the page (no ball playing, no skating, no bicycling). Then tell partners that they will brainstorm ideas for places where these signs should be placed for safety. They will complete the page by drawing one place for each sign.

4. Before they begin, ask partners to discuss ways to do the page together.
▪ Both children could contribute ideas.
▪ Children could take turns drawing pictures.
▪ One child could choose the ideas while the other draws them.

5. Encourage partners to draw other familiar signs or to create their own safety signs on the back of the page.

Focus on Cooperation Discuss brainstorming with the students. Do they think working with a partner helps them come up with more ideas? Does working together boost their creativity? How do they think brainstorming is helpful?

Name_____ Date_____

Name_____

Safety First!

NO BALL PLAYING   **NO SKATING**   **NO BICYCLING**

Look at these safety signs. Where should they go?
Draw a picture for each sign to show the places where
they would be needed.

Draw ☺ for yes. Draw ☹ for no.
Did you

speak quietly?

share ideas?

listen to each other?

Make a Map

Goals:
▪ Children will learn about map symbols by completing a street map.
▪ Children will practice taking turns, sharing materials, and sharing ideas.

What Each Pair Needs:
scissors
glue
crayons
Partners' Team-Up Sheet (page 11)
Make a Map reproducible (page 53)

What You Do:
1. Organize the class in pairs, giving one copy of the **Make a Map** reproducible page to each pair. Invite children to study the map, asking what it shows (streets in a neighborhood). Then focus attention on the map key. What do children think the map key is? Elicit from children that a map key explains the symbols used on a map. Talk about the meaning of each symbol shown: house, store, school, tree.

2. Place the materials where they can be shared. Invite children to complete their maps together by cutting out the symbols and pasting them in place. Encourage them to exchange ideas about how to color the map.

3. Remind children to work cooperatively by sharing materials, listening to ideas, and helping each other as needed.

4. Have partners compare their completed maps with classmates.

Focus on Cooperation Ask partners to write notes complimenting each other's work. The compliments should be specific. (For example, "Gina, I like that bright pink color you used.")

Name_____ Date_____

Name_____

Make a Map

Use the key and the symbols to complete this map.

Work together to follow these instructions:
1. Cut out all the map symbols.
2. Glue them on the map.
3. Draw more symbols, if you like.
4. Color the map.

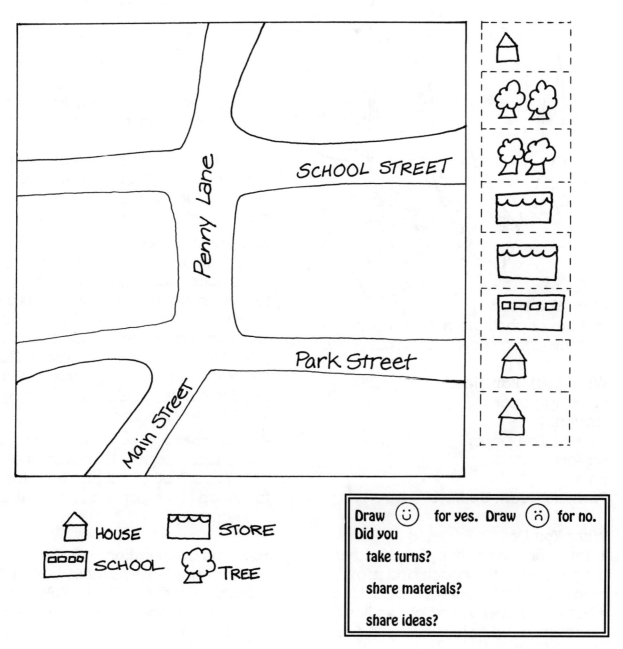

Draw ☺ for yes. Draw ☹ for no.
Did you
take turns?

share materials?

share ideas?

What Will We Bring?

Goals:
- **Children will practice thinking skills by planning what to take on an imaginary trip.**
- **Children will practice sharing ideas, being attentive listeners, and speaking courteously.**

What You Need:
pictures or photographs of a beach
   scene and a snowy mountain scene

What Each Pair Needs:
drawing paper
crayons
construction paper
scissors
tape
Partners' Team-Up Sheet (page 11)

What You Do:
1. Introduce the activity by displaying the pictures of the beach and snow scenes. Prompt discussion by asking:
- Have you ever visited places like the ones pictured here?

- What can you tell about the weather from looking at the pictures? (One place is warm, the other is cold.)
- What kinds of clothing might you need if you were traveling to a cold place? (hats, gloves, mittens, and so on) To a warm place? (bathing suit, T-shirts, shorts, and so on)

2. Group children in pairs and provide them with drawing paper and crayons. Tell the class that they will take a pretend journey and invite partners to decide whether to visit a warm place or a cold place. Ask them to brainstorm ideas for things to bring, especially the kinds of clothing they will need. Have children list or draw their ideas.

3. Then give each partner a sheet of drawing paper. Help them label the page horizontally, "My Suitcase." Explain that the paper represents the suitcase they will take on their journey. Ask each partner to choose items from the list to draw in the "suitcase." Have the partners compare papers and add any left-out items. Encourage them to label the items if they can.

4. Demonstrate how to cut an arc out of construction paper. Encourage partners to help each other cut and tape the arc to the top of the page to represent a suitcase handle.

Focus on Cooperation Ask the children if any disagreements arose during this activity. How were they resolved? How does being a good listener help resolve a disagreement?

A Neighborhood Museum

Goals:
▪ **Children will learn about museums by planning a museum for their neighborhood and making dioramas.**
▪ **Children will practice sharing materials, brainstorming ideas, and listening to their partners.**

What Each Pair Needs:
a carton or
  shoe box
construction paper
drawing paper
index cards
crayons/markers
glue
scissors
Partners' Team-Up Sheet (page 11)

What You Do:
1. Introduce the activity by writing the following announcement on the chalkboard:

Our Town Is Opening a New Museum

Read the announcement aloud. Then ask the children to pretend they have been called upon by the mayor (or other official) to plan the new museum.

2. Before they begin, encourage discussion of the different kinds of museums.
▪ Which kind of museum would you visit if you wanted to see paintings and sculptures?

▪ Which kind of museum would you visit if you wanted to see dinosaurs, rocks, and models of animals?

3. Pair students and place materials where they can be shared. Explain that partners will work together to choose a museum and to make a diorama showing one of its rooms. For example, if the children choose to make a natural history museum, the diorama may show a dinosaur exhibit.

4. Discuss with children how they might divide jobs.
▪ One partner could create the figure while the other places the figure within the diorama.
▪ Partners could decide which figures to include, then evenly split creating them.

5. Show children how to line the back and sides of the carton or shoe box with construction paper. Then demonstrate how to make a standing figure using a folded index card. Invite children to complete an exhibit for the museum of their choice, then present their dioramas to the class.

Focus on Cooperation Ask the children if they complimented each other as they worked. How do compliments make them feel? Why is it important to compliment one's partner?

A Paintbox of Our Own

Goals:
- Children will learn how primary colors are mixed to create paints of different colors.
- Children will practice taking turns and sharing materials.

What Each Pair Needs:
red, yellow, blue, and white
    tempera paints
cotton swabs
Partners' Team-Up Sheet (page 11)
A Paintbox of Our Own reproducible
    (page 57)

What You Do:
1. Let students work with partners, and arrange materials where everyone can use them.

2. Introduce the activity by discussing with students their experiences with painting and coloring. Challenge them to name some of the color words they might have seen on crayons: tulip pink, ocean blue, etc. Ask students how they think these colors are made. Then tell them they are going to work together to create colors of their own.

3. Show the class how to use cotton swabs to drip a little paint onto a sheet of paper. Demonstrate how to mix the drops to make a new color. Remind stu-

dents to use a fresh swab for the different paints.

4. Ask partner-pairs to discuss the different tasks involved before they begin.
- Partners take turns mixing colors.
- One partner fills in the paint colors on the reproducible page.
- One partner writes the new color names on the reproducible page.

5. Pass out one **A Paintbox of Our Own** reproducible page to each partner-pair and give the children time to create as many colors as they wish. Encourage them to experiment with different amounts of each paint to see how many colors they can make. On the reproducible page, make sure children name their new colors with color words they invent together.

Focus on Cooperation Ask the children how well they think they took turns and shared. How do taking turns and sharing contribute to doing a better job?

Name_____ Date_____

Name_____

A Paintbox of Our Own

What new colors did you make? Work together to name the new colors in your paintbox.

1. Fill in each space with a color that you made.

2. Write the name for your new paint color.

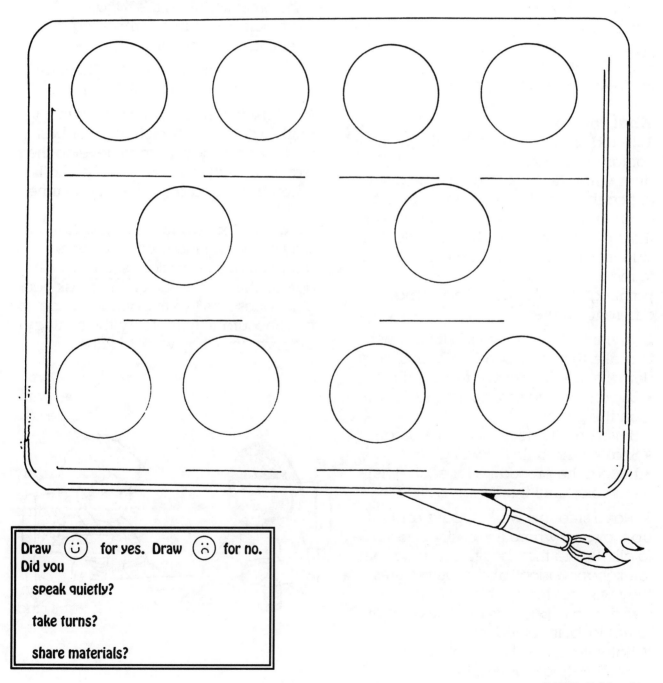

Draw 🙂 for yes. Draw 🙁 for no.
Did you

speak quietly?

take turns?

share materials?

Sand Art

Goals:
- **Children will use sand of different colors to create sand pictures.**
- **Children will practice taking turns, sharing materials, and exchanging ideas.**

What Each Pair Needs:
small containers of sand in assorted colors (if pre-colored sand is not available, plain sand can be colored with food dye)
white glue
a paintbrush
9" x 12" oaktag sheets
Partners' Team-Up Sheet (page 11)

What You Do:
1. Introduce the activity by displaying containers of colored sand. Ask children what they notice about the different containers. (The sand in each one is a different color.) Let volunteers touch the sand and describe how it feels. Tell students that colored sand can be used to make pictures. Explain that "sand painting" is an old art found in many different cultures.

2. Invite children to work with partners to make their own sand paintings. First, demonstrate the art of sand painting.
- Use a pencil to draw a simple design on the paper.
- Brush on glue to fill one color area.
- Shake sand onto the wet glue.
- Repeat the procedure for each different color until the design is filled in.

3. Have students work in pairs and set up the sand where it is easily accessible to all. Before they begin, invite partners to exchange ideas about the pictures they wish to draw. Once that has been decided, ask partners to discuss the different tasks involved in the project. What will their first step be? How will they share the different tasks?

- One partner draws the picture while the other collects the colored sand needed.
- As one partner brushes on the glue, the other sprinkles the sand.
- Partners take turns completing a section of the picture.

Give one **Partners' Team-Up Sheet** to each pair and help children fill it in.

4. Set aside time for children to work in pairs to create their pictures. For best results encourage them to develop the pictures slowly and to use only small amounts of sand and glue at one time.

Focus on Cooperation Suggest that one way of sharing ideas is for partners to ask each other questions such as, "What do you think?" Did the children ask each other questions like this during the activity? Encourage them to try this strategy the next time they work together.

Stencil Fun

Goals:
- **Children will use stencils to create patterned wrapping paper.**
- **Children will practice sharing materials and ideas.**

What You Need:
5" oaktag squares or index cards
pencils
scissors

What Each Pair Needs:
a prepared stencil
paint
small sponge squares
newsprint
Partners' Team-Up Sheet (page 11)

What You Do:

1. In advance, prepare stencils for children to use. Draw and cut out shapes from oaktag or index cards.

2. Gather children together to watch carefully as you demonstrate and describe how to use a stencil.
- Place the stencil firmly on the newsprint.
- Dip the sponge lightly in the paint.
- Cover the stencil shape and a bit of the surrounding area with paint.

- Lift the stencil off without smudging.
- Repeat several times to make the pattern.

Tell children that patterned paper can be used for wrapping paper.

3. Pair students and place materials where they can be shared. Distribute one **Partners' Team-Up Sheet** to each pair to fill out.

4. Give the partner-pairs time to work together to create several sheets of wrapping paper. Encourage them to confer about which stencil shape to use. Suggest that children work with other partner-pairs to trade stencils and try to create stencils of their own.

Focus on Cooperation Ask the children how well they shared the stencils. Did any problems arise? If so, ask a partner-pair to role-play the problem. Then invite the class to discuss how the problem could be solved.

Imagine That!

Goals:
▪ Children will create mobiles with shapes and glitter.
▪ Children will practice taking turns, sharing materials, and listening to partners.

What Each Pair Needs:
scissors
white glue
sheets of oaktag
assorted colors of glitter in easy-to-use
  containers
hole puncher
string
wire hanger
Partners' Team-Up Sheet (page 11)
Imagine That! reproducibles (page 61)

What You Do:
1. Arrange students in pairs and give one copy of the **Imagine That!** reproducible page to each child. Challenge children to name the shapes they see (triangle, square, circle, and star). Tell children that with these simple shapes and their imaginations, they will create a mobile with their partners. Review with children that a mobile is a hang-ing sculpture that moves and bal-ances.

2. Demonstrate the following steps in making this mobile.
▪ Glue the **Imagine That!** reproducible page to a sheet of oaktag. Cut out the shapes.
▪ Spread glue over the shape or dribble it in lines to form a design.
▪ Shake glitter onto wet glue.
▪ Repeat for each shape.
▪ Use the hole puncher to make a hole at the top of each shape.
▪ Attach the shape with string to the hanger.

3. Place materials where they can be shared and remind children to use all their cutouts to complete the mobile.

4. Discuss with partners how they might help each other and list their ideas on the chalkboard. These might include:
▪ cutting out shapes
▪ spreading glue
▪ shaking on glitter
▪ stringing shapes to the mobile
Encourage children to talk over what their first step should be.

5. Now invite children to work in pairs to create their mobiles. Encourage them to take their time and to listen to and acknowledge each other's ideas.

Focus on Cooperation Remind students to review the **Ways to Act with a Partner** list on page 8. Which of the ways to act was most helpful for this activity?

Imagine That!

Use these shapes to make a fancy mobile.

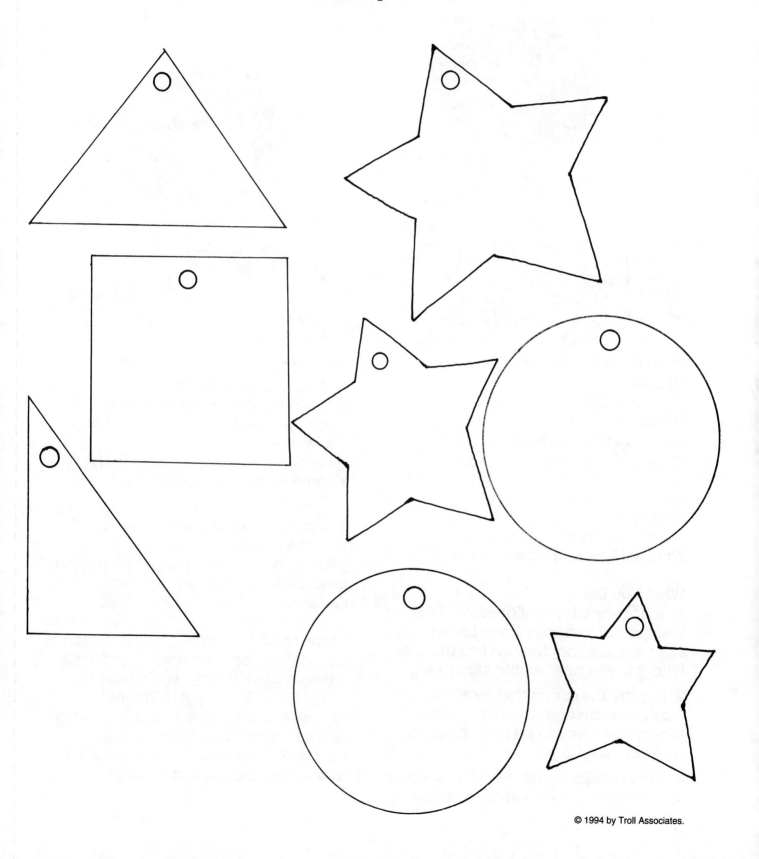

Playful Pets

Goals:
▪ Children will create "playful pets" from a variety of materials.
▪ Children will practice sharing materials and ideas.

What Each Pair Needs:
cardboard tubes
pipe cleaners
cotton balls
craft eyes (if available)
construction paper
tape
glue
scissors
crayons/markers
Partners' Team-Up Sheet (page 11)

What You Do:
1. Start by inviting children to talk about their pets or pets they have known. Then explain that they will create pretend "playful pets" for the classroom.

2. Display the assembled materials. Challenge children to think of ways that these materials can be put together to make a "playful pet."

3. After grouping children with partners, seat them in a common area where

they can easily use all materials.

4. Before they begin, ask partners to discuss the different tasks involved:
▪ sharing ideas about what kind of pet to make
▪ taking turns adding details to the pet
▪ cutting materials and gluing them to their pet

5. Encourage children to experiment with the materials to create different "playful pets." Have partner-pairs share their creations and display them in the classroom.

Focus on Cooperation Encourage partner-pairs to compare how they decided which materials they would use to make their playful pets. Did they always agree? Did they talk over why one material would be better than another? Why do they think conferring about their plans is worthwhile?

At the Card Shop

Goals:
- **Students will write messages or verses for their own collection of greeting cards.**
- **Students will practice sharing tasks and responsibilities.**

Suggested number of students in each group: 4
Suggested jobs: Guide, Recorder, Booster, Reporter

What You Need:
greeting card samples

What Each Team Needs:
folded drawing paper
crayons/markers
Team-Up Sheet (page 15)
appropriate **Job Sheets** (pages 16, 17, 19, and 21)

What You Do:
1. Introduce the activity by presenting the class with a selection of different greeting cards and discussing different occasions for sending them. What kinds of cards have children seen at a card shop?

2. Invite volunteers to take turns reading the greeting-card messages aloud and note any rhythm or rhyme patterns. Point out that greetings may or may not rhyme and can be humorous or serious, depending on the occasion. Also call attention to the card design. Guide children to conclude that both the message and the design are important.

3. Now tell children they will work in teams to create their own greeting-card collections. Discuss the different jobs involved:
- choosing categories for which to make cards
- writing down verses and messages the team makes up
- printing verses neatly on the cards
- making designs and illustrations
- revising and editing each other's writings

4. Divide the class into groups of four. Before they begin, distribute copies of the **Team-Up Sheet** and the appropriate **Job Sheets** for students to complete. Place materials where they can be shared.

5. Suggest that groups start off by brainstorming a list of different kinds of cards, making sure the Recorder writes down their ideas. What kinds of cards will they create? What will the messages say? Encourage students to experiment with rhyming and non-rhyming messages. Set aside time for groups to create as many cards as they wish.

6. When groups' card collections are complete, ask the Reporters to read aloud several cards. Just for fun, you might save the cards for a class card sale.

Focus on Cooperation Invite students to talk about how well they worked together. Did any problems arise? How were they solved? How might children work together better next time?

Think Thesaurus!

Goals:
- Students will use a thesaurus to help revise a familiar fable.
- Students will practice sharing materials, being good listeners, and sharing ideas.

Suggested number of students in each group: 3
Suggested jobs: Guide, Recorder, Reporter

What You Need:
a copy of the Aesop's fable "The Lion and the Mouse"

What Each Team Needs:
pencils
a student thesaurus
Team-Up Sheet (page 15)
appropriate **Job Sheets** (pages 16, 17, and 21)
Think Thesaurus! reproducible (page 65)

What You Do:
1. Share with the class the familiar fable "The Lion and the Mouse." Then write these sentences about the fable on the chalkboard:

The mouse was nice.
The lion was nice.
I enjoyed this nice fable.

Ask children which word describes the mouse, the lion, and the fable. Erase the word "nice" in each sentence and ask children to suggest other describing words or adjectives that tell more about the mouse, the lion, and the fable. Complete the sentences using students' suggestions. Do students think the new sentences tell more about the story? Are the sentences less repetitive? Why do the students think so?

2. Now display a copy of a thesaurus. Review with students that entries, or words, are in alphabetical order and synonyms are provided for each entry. (Review that synonyms are words that have the same or almost the same meanings.) Ask students to tell how a thesaurus could be useful to a writer.

3. Divide the children into groups of three and give one copy of the **Think Thesaurus!** reproducible page to each team. Invite a student to read the directions aloud. Tell children that they will work with their teammates to complete the page using the thesaurus as a resource. Encourage teammates to discuss their choices, letting the Recorder write down the words they agree create a more interesting version of the fable "The Fox and the Grapes."

4. Also distribute copies of the **Team-Up Sheet** and the appropriate **Job Sheets** for students to complete.

5. When ready, ask the Reporters to read aloud the revised fable so classmates can appreciate the changes.

Focus on Cooperation Talk about how sharing ideas and being good listeners go together. Encourage students to explain how they made their decisions about which words to use.

Name_____ Date_____

Name_____

Name_____

Think Thesaurus!

Make this version of "The Fox and the Grapes" more interesting.
Work together to think of new words or find the words you need
in a thesaurus.

1. As you read the story, you will notice that some words are crossed out.

2. Use a ∧ and write another describing word to replace each crossed-out word.
Be careful! Don't use the same word more than one time.

The Fox and the Grapes

Once upon a time, a wandering fox was very hungry. He saw a
~~beautiful~~ grape vine on the other side of the river, and he decided
to cross the ~~big~~ river to reach the ~~beautiful~~ vine. When he got to
the other side, he looked up at the fine grapes. How ~~nice~~ they
looked! They will make a ~~good~~ treat! So the fox jumped to try
and reach those ~~nice~~ grapes. But though he tried and
tried, he could not quite reach them.

Finally, he took another long look at the sweet
grapes, and he said, "Oh, well. They were probably
sour anyway!" And off went the almost happy,
though hungry, wandering fox.

Write a ✔
Today our group practiced
sharing materials_____
being good listeners_____
sharing ideas_____

Invent a Game

Goals:
- Students will write rules and instructions for a board game they invent themselves.
- Students will practice sharing ideas, asking questions, and listening to group members.

Suggested number of students in each group: 4
Suggested jobs: Guide, Recorder, Checker, Organizer

What Each Team Needs:
pencils
10 index cards
small playing pieces (colored chips or cubes)
one die
Team-Up Sheet (page 15)
appropriate **Job Sheets** (pages 16, 17, 18, and 20)
Invent a Game reproducibles (page 67)

What You Do:
1. Divide the class into groups of four. Introduce the activity by asking group members to name some familiar board games. Ask students to discuss in their groups what most games have in common (a game board, direction cards, player pieces, dice).

2. Distribute several copies of the **Invent a Game** reproducible page to each group. Explain to the children that they will create their own game using the blank game board on the page. Help

them locate the "Start" and the "Winner" squares.

3. Write these steps on the chalkboard and review them.
- Work together to fill in the spaces on the board with names of different places. The places can be real or made up.
- Write direction cards using the following terms:
  Go ahead ____ spaces.
  Go back ____ spaces.
  Lose a turn.

4. Then provide each group with game pieces, one die, and index cards for writing directions. Encourage students to suggest other ways of making the game more elaborate.

5. Ask students to discuss how they will share the work. To help them, distribute copies of the **Team-Up Sheet** and the appropriate **Job Sheets**.

6. As they work, encourage students to experiment with several ideas. Have them play the games they create, revising to make them longer, shorter, or more interesting. If time allows, have teams try out each other's games.

Focus on Cooperation Suggest that one way of sharing ideas is for teammates to ask each other questions and to listen to each other's answers. Did students ask each other questions during this activity? Did it help to clarify things? Encourage them to work this way in subsequent activities.

Date_____

Name_____   Name_____

Name_____   Name_____

Invent a Game

Work together to create your own board game. Then play the game together.

AS ...
AS ...

Goals:
- Students will practice using similes by compiling pages for a book of similes.
- Students will practice sharing ideas, being attentive listeners, and giving compliments.

Suggested number of students in each group: 6

Suggested jobs: Guide, Recorder, Checker, Booster, Organizer, Reporter

What Each Team Needs:
pencils
crayons/markers
drawing paper
stapler
Team-Up Sheet (page 15)
appropriate **Job Sheets** (pages 16-21)

What You Do:

1. Divide the class into groups of six. Start by writing the following similes on the chalkboard, and invite a volunteer to read them aloud.

"as quiet as a mouse"
"as dark as night"
"as fast as lightning"

2. Challenge students to figure out what all these phrases have in common. (They all describe something using the word "as.") Explain that phrases like

these are called *similes* and that writers use similes to make their descriptions more vivid. Then have teams discuss what things a writer might describe as being "as fast as lightning" (a rocket, a racing car, a runner). Invite children to illustrate their suggestions on the chalkboard below the similes.

3. Discuss the things each group will need to do to create their own book of similes. For example:
- brainstorming and recording a list of similes
- choosing which similes to use in the booklet
- illustrating each simile
- revising and editing each other's work

4. Before students begin, distribute copies of the **Team-Up Sheet** and the appropriate **Job Sheets** for students to fill out.

5. Now challenge teams to create booklets of similes and to illustrate them. Encourage teams to use similes they know or to make up similes of their own.

6. Invite groups to share their completed simile books with another class or to have them displayed in the school library.

Focus on Cooperation Discuss brainstorming with the class. How does working as part of a team help to gather more ideas? How are listening and sharing ideas part of brainstorming?

Our Dream Catalog

Goals:
- **Students will write descriptions of objects for a "dream catalog."**
- **Students will practice sharing materials, exchanging ideas, and speaking politely.**

Suggested number of students in each group: 6

Suggested jobs: Guide, Recorder, Checker, Booster, Organizer, Reporter

What You Need:
catalogs

What Each Team Needs:
magazines
scissors
glue
crayons/markers
drawing paper
stapler
Team-Up Sheet (page 15)
appropriate **Job Sheets** (pages 16-21)

What You Do:
1. Divide the class into groups of six. Write the following catalog description on the chalkboard:

> **Easy to fly, blue-and-white striped diamond-shaped kite. Just what you need to enjoy a breezy day in the park. Price: $7.99**

Discuss the different elements of the description. Note that it tells the kite's colors and shape, how it might be used, and the price. Ask children if the description would encourage them to buy the kite.

2. Now display several catalogs and invite volunteers to read aloud several descriptions. Explain to children that they will work with their teams to create their own catalog called "Our Dream Catalog." Tell them they can cut pictures of their items from magazines, or they can simply draw them.

3. Give the team members time to plan the things they will need to do:
- choosing items to include in their catalog
- cutting and pasting magazine illustrations onto drawing paper
- drawing catalog items
- writing descriptions of each catalog item
- pricing their catalog items
- revising and editing their catalog

4. To help children get started, distribute copies of the **Team-Up Sheet** and the appropriate **Job Sheets**. Seat groups where they can share materials.

5. As children work, encourage them to discuss why each item should be included in their dream catalog. Do they all agree? Help children resolve arguments if necessary. Suggest that students share their dream catalogs and make "dream purchases."

Focus on Cooperation Ask students to evaluate how sharing ideas and materials contributes to making the activity more successful.

Believe It or Not!

Goals:
- Students will research animal facts to complete an animal trivia list.
- Students will practice discussing ideas, sharing materials, asking questions, and being good listeners.

Suggested number of students in each group: 5

Suggested jobs: Guide, Recorder, Checker, Organizer, Reporter

What Each Team Needs:
resource material on animals, such as books of animal records, encyclopedias, non-fiction books

Team-Up Sheet (page 15)

appropriate **Job Sheets** (pages 16, 17, 18, 20, and 21)

Believe It or Not! reproducibles (page 71)

What You Do:
1. Assign students to groups of five. Begin by asking students if they've ever played games of trivia. What are trivia? (unusual, little-known facts of varying importance) Then explain that students will have a chance to find and use trivia facts about animals. Distribute a **Believe It or Not!** reproducible page to each student in a group.

2. Have a volunteer read aloud the directions and explain that, although students may know some of the answers, others will have to be researched, either in the library or with resources you have collected. Children will need to work with their teammates to research the information. Emphasize that they should compare and discuss their findings as they work so that all teammates have the same answers.

3. Place research materials in a central work area. Before students begin, distribute copies of the **Team-Up Sheet** and appropriate **Job Sheets** for them to complete.

4. Then invite groups to research their animal trivia facts. When all the teams are finished, gather the groups to share results. Discuss any discrepancies and have groups research further if necessary.

Focus on Cooperation Discuss with students the benefits of sharing ideas and materials when doing research assignments. Why is it important for researchers to ask questions and listen to each other?

Answers to "Believe It or Not!" reproducible: 1. 100; 2. arachnids; 3. meat; 4. 70; 5. 150; 6. claws; 7. sailfish; 8. a garden snail; 9. 300; 10. mammal; 11. color; 12. seal

Believe It or Not!

Read each fact and circle the correct answer.

1. Elephants' tusks can weigh _____ pounds.

   3   500   100

2. Spiders are not insects. They are _____ .

   arachnids   archaeologists
   amoebas

3. Horses do not eat _____ .

   oats   grass   meat

4. The cheetah is the fastest animal and can run _____ miles per hour.

   30   40   70

5. Some turtles can live as long as _____ years.

   150   20   100

6. Crabs can grow new _____ .

   eyes   wings   claws

7. The fastest swimming fish is the _____ .

   tuna   sailfish   sunfish

8. The slowest animal is_____ .

   an earthworm   a rattlesnake
   a garden snail

9. Insects first appeared on earth _____ million years ago.

   10   50   300

10. Even though a platypus has a bill like a bird, it is really a

   _____ .

   reptile   amphibian
   mammal

11. A chameleon can change its

   _____ .

   color   life cycle   shape

12. A young dog is called a "pup" and so is a young _____ .

   deer   seal   horse

Write a ✔
Today our group practiced
sharing ideas _____
sharing materials_____
asking questions _____
being good listeners _____

Recycling Reminders

Goals:
- Students will learn the importance of recycling by writing recycling reminders.
- Students will practice using materials together and giving compliments.

Suggested number of students in each group: 6
Suggested jobs: Guide, Recorder, Checker, Booster, Organizer, Reporter

What Each Team Needs:
resource materials on recycling
index cards
crayons/markers
Team-Up Sheet (page 15)
appropriate **Job Sheets** (pages 16-21)

What You Do:
1. Introduce the activity with a discussion about the recycling programs in your school, community, and/or city. Talk about the importance of recycling and write students' ideas on the chalkboard.

2. Then explain that students will be working in groups to write recycling reminders on index cards for their families and friends. Suggest that they decorate the border of each index card with a magic marker, then write the recycling reminder. For example, one such reminder might be: Remember to rinse glass bottles and jars before putting them in recycling bins.

3. Place materials where they can be shared and divide the class into groups of six. Distribute copies of the **Team-Up Sheet** and appropriate **Job Sheets** for groups to complete.

4. Encourage students to begin by brainstorming a list of recycling rules with their teammates, asking the Recorder to jot down group members' suggestions. Refer students to resource materials for more ideas.

5. When groups are satisfied with their work, invite the Reporters to share their recycling tips with the class. Display the completed recycling reminders in a school hallway for others to learn from. At a later time, let children take them home as reminders to family members to recycle properly.

Focus on Cooperation Ask students to recall compliments they received from their teammates while working together. How do compliments make them feel? Why is it important to compliment one's teammates?

Animal, Vegetable, or Mineral?

Goals:
- Students will learn science facts by playing a science guessing game.
- Students will practice taking turns, being good listeners, and speaking quietly.

Suggested number of students in each group: 4

Note: Because of the nature of this activity, the traditional cooperative learning roles are not necessary.

What Each Team Needs:
paper
pencils

What You Do:
1. Ask students to share their experiences playing guessing games. Has anyone ever played the game "Twenty Questions," which is sometimes called "Animal, Vegetable, Mineral"? Ask volunteers to explain the rules of the game or explain them as follows:

- The person who is "It" thinks of an object for the others to guess.
- The group members then ask if the object is an animal, vegetable, or mineral.
- The guessers take turns asking questions that can be answered with either "Yes" or "No."
- The scorekeeper keeps track of how many questions have been asked and stops the group at twenty questions. If the guessers have been stumped, "It" gives the answer.
- Another person becomes "It" and the game continues.

2. Before students play, talk about the different categories for the game. All kinds of animals—from fish to insects to birds to mammals—are classed as "ani- mal." All kinds of plants—from fruits to flowers to trees to weeds—are classed as "vegetable." Anything formed by nature that is not "animal" or "vegetable" is classed as "mineral," as are items made from them, such as a ring, a toaster, etc.

3. Divide the class into groups of four. Give the groups time to plan who will start as "It," who will be scorekeeper, and how jobs will rotate.

4. Allow time for teams to play so that every child gets a turn to be "It."

Focus on Cooperation Talk about why it is important to speak quietly when playing games in teams at school. Discuss what might have happened if everyone spoke loudly.

Are You an Amphibian?

Goals:
- ▪ Students will learn some characteristics of amphibians.
- ▪ Students will practice taking turns, exchanging ideas, and sharing materials.

**Suggested number
of students in each group:** 3
Suggested jobs: Checker, Booster, Organizer

What Each Team Needs:
pencils
resource materials on animals, such as
   dictionaries, encyclopedias, non-fiction
   books
Team-Up Sheet (page 15)
appropriate **Job Sheets** (pages 18-20)
Are You an Amphibian? reproducible
   (page 75)

What You Do:
1. Let students work in groups of three. Introduce the activity by asking groups to list animals that live and breathe underwater. Then ask them to list animals that can live only on land.

2. Explain that certain animals breathe underwater for only part of their lives. Explain that as babies, these animals live in water and breathe through gills, like fish. But as they grow, they develop lungs to breathe air. They then must live mainly on land. These animals are called amphibians. Can groups name any? (frog, salamander, newt, toad) Tell children they will complete a word search to find out which animals are amphibians.

3. Start by distributing copies of the **Team-Up Sheet** and the appropriate **Job Sheets** to each team.

4. Then distribute one copy of the **Are You an Amphibian?** reproducible page to each group. Provide dictionaries or other resource materials, encouraging team members to refer to them as needed.

5. When groups have completed the activity, gather the teams together to share results. Did everyone come up with frog, toad, newt, and salamander? Ask if any children have ever owned or observed these animals. Invite them to share their experiences with amphibians.

Focus on Cooperation Ask the group to evaluate how well they were able to avoid distractions and stay on task.

Answers to "Are You an Amphibian?" page 75: ~~dog~~ ~~lamb~~ newt ~~lion~~ ~~goat~~ frog ~~elephant~~ ~~bear~~ salamander toad

Name_____ Date_____

Name_____

Name_____

Are You an Amphibian?

There are 10 animal names in this puzzle, but only four are amphibians! Work together to find them all.

1. Circle all the animal names. List the animals on the lines.

_____   _____   _____

_____   _____   _____

_____   _____   _____

_____

2. Now look at your list. Cross out the name of any animal that does not begin life in the water. If you are not sure, use the reference books to help you.

3. Which four animals are not crossed out? You have found the amphibians!

4. On the back of this sheet, write the name of at least one amphibian and draw a picture of it.

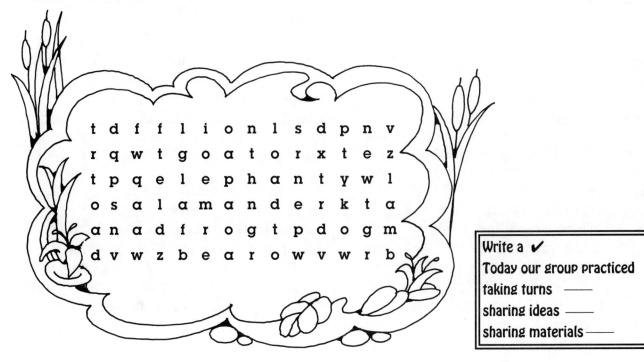

```
t  d  f  f  l  i  o  n  l  s  d  p  n  v
r  q  w  t  g  o  a  t  o  r  x  t  e  z
t  p  q  e  l  e  p  h  a  n  t  y  w  l
o  s  a  l  a  m  a  n  d  e  r  k  t  a
a  n  a  d  f  r  o  g  t  p  d  o  g  m
d  v  w  z  b  e  a  r  o  w  v  w  r  b
```

Write a ✔
Today our group practiced
taking turns ——
sharing ideas ——
sharing materials ——

Measure Up

Goals:
▪ **Students will measure classroom objects.**
▪ **Students will practice taking turns, sharing materials, and speaking quietly.**

Suggested number of students in each group: 3
Suggested jobs: Recorder, Checker, Organizer

What Each Team Needs:
items to use as measuring tools, such as six-inch lengths of string, spaghetti sticks, craft sticks, six-inch rulers, paper clips
pencils
Team-Up Sheet (page 15)
appropriate **Job Sheets** (pages 17, 18, 20)
Measure Up reproducible (page 77)

What You Do:
1. Gather the children around a central work area displaying a collection of spaghetti sticks, craft sticks, paper clips, rulers, and six-inch lengths of string. Ask a volunteer to choose one item to use to "measure" the length of a desk. Demonstrate how to find out how many lengths of that object equals the length of the desk. Point out that before rulers, people measured items using hands, feet, and arms.
2. Tell children they will have a chance

to measure things around the room using the different items. Divide children into groups of three and pass out a copy of the **Measure Up** reproducible page to each team.

3. Get children started by having the teams decide how they will organize this activity. Distribute copies of the **Team-Up Sheet** and **Job Sheets** for students to complete.

4. Now ask children to work with their teammates to complete the **Measure Up** reproducible page using the different measuring tools. Set aside a specific amount of time for children to complete the activity. Conclude by inviting teams to share results with other groups.

Focus on Cooperation Have students evaluate how well they were able to work quietly. Was everyone in the group able to hear his or her teammates? Did the noise of other groups hinder work? Were groups able to complete their tasks within the given time limits?

Name_____ Date_____

Name_____

Name_____

Measure Up

Try each item as a measuring tool. Write your numbers on the lines.

Measure a desk.

_____ spaghetti sticks

_____ craft sticks

_____ inches

Measure a book.

_____ paper clips

_____ craft sticks

_____ inches

Measure a sheet of paper.

_____ paper clips

_____ strings

_____ inches

Measure a pencil.

_____ string(s)

_____ craft sticks

_____ inches

Measure a crayon.

_____ paper clips

_____ string

_____ inches

Measure the window ledge.

_____ strings

_____ inches

_____ spaghetti sticks

Write a ✔
Today our group practiced
taking turns _____
sharing materials _____

Amazing Mazes

Goals:
- Students will use geometric shapes to create their own mazes.
- Students will practice taking turns, discussing ideas, and sharing materials.

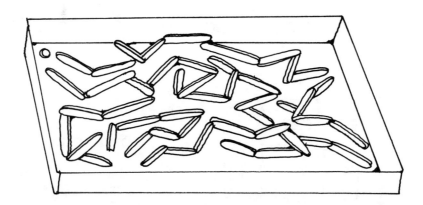

Suggested number of students in each group: 3

Suggested jobs: Guide, Checker, Organizer

What You Need:
hand-held maze games to show as samples

What Each Team Needs:
cardboard box lid
construction paper
glue
craft sticks
marbles
Team-Up Sheet (page 15)
appropriate **Job Sheets** (pages 16, 18, and 20)

What You Do:
1. To introduce the activity, display several simple hand-held maze games. (If not available, ask students to describe hand-held maze games that they have played with.) Ask students to notice the geometric shapes that make up the maze. Have them explain the object of a maze or maze game.

2. Divide the class into groups of three and place materials where they can be shared. Challenge groups to come up with a way to put together these materials into geometric shapes to create a maze.

3. Discuss the different steps students might follow.
- Line a cardboard box with construction paper.
- Place craft sticks (or doubled craft sticks) to make paths.
- Test the game to see if it works.
- Glue in craft sticks.
Encourage students to experiment with many different layouts.

4. Hand out copies of the **Team-Up Sheet** and appropriate **Job Sheets**.

5. Now let groups construct their mazes. Invite teams to share their completed mazes and keep them in the classroom for children to enjoy.

Focus on Cooperation Ask teammates to evaluate how effectively they divided the tasks for this activity. Would they do anything differently if they participated in the activity again?

Code and Decode

Goals:
- Students will practice manipulating symbols by creating codes and decoding messages.
- Students will practice speaking kindly and politely.

Suggested number of students in each group: 3
Suggested jobs: Guide, Recorder, Checker

What Each Team Needs:
paper
pencils
Team-Up Sheet (page 15)
appropriate **Job Sheets** (pages 16-18)

What You Do:
1. Begin by asking students to share their experiences creating codes or deciphering messages. Then explain that one of the simplest codes is one that matches alphabet letters with numbers. Write the following code chart on the chalkboard:

A	B	C	D	E	F	G	H	I	J	K	L	M
1	2	3	4	5	6	7	8	9	10	11	12	13

N	O	P	Q	R	S	T	U	V	W	X	Y	Z
14	15	16	17	18	19	20	21	22	23	24	25	26

Print the following coded message and challenge children to decode it:

9   3,1,14   18,5,1,4   20,8,9,19
(I can read this)

2. Then explain that sometimes decoding a message can be more complicated, and give the following example:

6 + 3
2 + 1, 3 - 2, 7 + 7,
9 + 9, 10 - 5, 0 + 1, 8 - 4
10 + 10, 4 + 4, 10 - 1, 20 - 1

3. How do students think this message can be solved? Elicit ideas, then have students decode the message. (I can read this) Choose a volunteer to write the word <u>code</u> using this addition or subtraction technique.

4. Leave the code chart on the chalkboard for students to refer to. Divide the class into groups of three and explain that students will create messages for their teammates to decode.

5. Before they begin, distribute copies of the **Team-Up Sheet** and appropriate **Job Sheets** for students to complete.

6. When the teammates are ready, have them trade papers to decode each other's secret messages.

Focus on Cooperation Talk about why it is important for partners to speak kindly and politely to each other. What should you do if you disagree with your team? Encourage children to practice giving constructive criticism.

Collectors All

Goals:
- Students will complete a graph and make up word problems for classmates to solve.
- Students will practice sharing materials, taking turns, and speaking courteously.

**Suggested number
of students in each group:** 4
Suggested jobs: Guide, Recorder,
Checker, Reporter

What Each Team Needs:
paper
pencils
Team-Up Sheet (page 15)
appropriate **Job Sheets** (pages 16, 17,
  18, and 21)
Collectors All reproducible (page 81)

What You Do:
1. Invite children to share the kinds of
items they like to collect. Point out that
people like to collect many different
things.

2. Divide the class into groups of four
and give one copy of the **Collectors All**
reproducible page to each group. Have
a volunteer read the directions aloud.
Focus attention on the pictures that
show what each child collects, explaining that the collections provide the information needed for making a bar graph.

3. Explain that after students help each
other complete the graph, groups will
work together to write three word problems based on the graph's information.
For example: "How many more items
does Melissa have in her collection than
Sam?" "If Emily collects 32 more stickers,
how many will she have in all?"

4. Help students begin by distributing
copies of the **Team-Up Sheet** and the
appropriate **Job Sheets** for students to
complete.

5. Now challenge groups to make their
graphs and to be creative when writing
their word problems. When ready,
have teams trade papers and solve
each other's problems.

Focus on Cooperation Review the list of
Cooperation Skills (see page 13).
Determine which skills were most help-
ful for this activity.

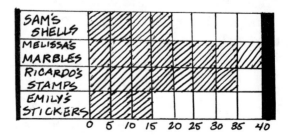

Date_____

Name_____ Name_____

Name_____ Name_____

Collectors All

Each child is starting a collection. How many things do they have?
Work together to complete the graph.

 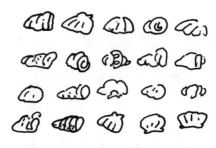

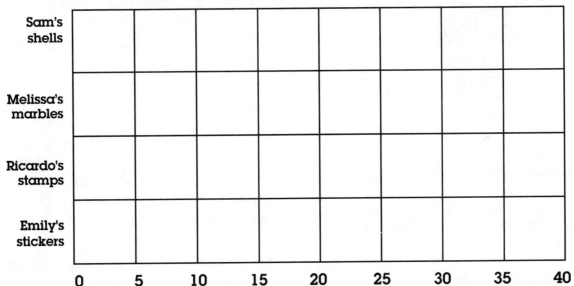

Sam's shells								
Melissa's marbles								
Ricardo's stamps								
Emily's stickers								

0   5   10   15   20   25   30   35   40

┌─────────────────────────────┐
│ Write a ✔   │
│ Today our group practiced   │
│ sharing materials ____   │
│ taking turns ____   │
│ speaking kindly ____   │
│ speaking politely ____   │
└─────────────────────────────┘

Best Jelly Bean Contest Ever

Goals:
- Students will estimate the number of jelly beans in jars of various sizes and shapes.
- Students will practice taking turns, talking softly, and listening to teammates.

Suggested number of students in each group: 6

Note: Because of the nature of this activity, the traditional cooperative learning roles are not necessary.

What Each Team Needs:

a one-pound bag of jelly beans
empty baby-food jars and other
  assorted small containers
scrap paper
pencils

What You Do:

1. Fill a small jar or container with jelly beans. Pass out several pieces of scrap paper and ask volunteers to guess, or "estimate," the number of beans in the jar. Record students' predictions on the chalkboard. Then empty the jar and count the beans to see whose guess was closest.

2. Divide the class into groups of six, explaining that they will work as a team to come up with one guess. Refill the jar from the bag of jelly beans and repeat the activity. Point out that it might be wise to choose numbers close to the previous number of jelly beans. Ask groups to select one member to offer their guesses. Record groups' estimates and determine which group's guess was closest.

3. Now challenge groups to make their own jelly-bean guessing jars. Ask group members to take turns filling a jar or container, handing out scrap paper, collecting guesses, counting the beans, and checking whose prediction was closest. You might have groups compete against each other as they continue with each round of guessing.

4. Encourage students to experiment with estimating and predicting. Suggest that teams make guesses based on the size and shape of each container and that they use previous guesses as guides.

Focus on Cooperation Ask teammates to rate their enjoyment of this activity, indicating "fair," "good," or "excellent," by a show of hands. Did working together make the activity more enjoyable? Why or why not? Did they like having the teams compete?

Rain Forest Treasure

Goals:
▪ Students will learn about the variety of animal life that lives in the canopy of a tropical rain forest.
▪ Students will practice sharing materials, exchanging ideas, and being attentive listeners.

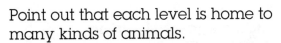

Suggested number of students in each group: 6
Suggested jobs: Guide, Recorder, Checker, Booster, Organizer, Reporter

What Each Team Needs:
resource materials on the rain forest, such as non-fiction children's books, encyclopedias, animal fact books
markers/crayons
drawing paper
scissors
green construction paper
glue
mural paper
Team-Up Sheet (page 15)
appropriate **Job Sheets** (pages 16-21)

What You Do:
1. Help children locate the Amazon rain forest on a map of South America. Ask students to share what they know about the dangers of destroying vast portions of the rain forest: the extinction of plant and animal life, the destruction of plants that may provide medicines to cure diseases, the elimination of trees that make oxygen for the earth, etc.

2. Then present children with a diagram of the three levels of the rain forest:

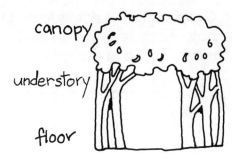

Point out that each level is home to many kinds of animals.

3. Now divide the class into groups of six. Tell children they will work in teams to create a mural of animals that live in the canopy of the Amazon rain forest. Encourage students to use the resources you've provided. Discuss the different jobs involved:
▪ researching information
▪ locating pictures of animals
▪ drawing pictures of animals
▪ making cutouts of animals
▪ labeling animal pictures
▪ creating a "canopy" background out of green construction paper
▪ pasting the animal cutouts onto the "canopy"

4. Place materials where they can be shared and distribute copies of the **Team-Up Sheet** and the appropriate **Job Sheets** for students to complete.

5. When the murals are complete, invite groups to compare them.

Focus on Cooperation Ask students to report on and evaluate the ways they found to share materials and divide tasks in this activity.

The Great State of ____

Goals:
- Students will learn facts about a state by creating a chart.
- Students will practice sharing materials, talking over ideas, and speaking quietly.

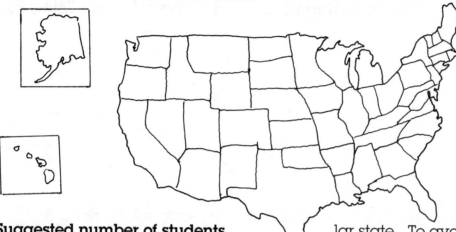

Suggested number of students in each group: 3
Suggested jobs: Guide, Recorder, Reporter

What Each Team Needs:
resource materials on states, such as non-fiction books, encyclopedias, and dictionaries
pencils
crayons/markers
Team-Up Sheet (page 15)
appropriate **Job Sheets** (pages 16, 17, and 21)
The Great State of ____ reproducible (page 85)

What You Do:
1. To introduce the activity, display a map of the United States. Invite volunteers to locate states they have visited or where they have friends or relatives. Review with children that each state has its own state capital as well as its own nickname, state bird, state flower, and state tree.

2. Divide the class into groups of three. Tell children they will work with teammates to collect facts about one particu-

lar state. To avoid duplication, you might have children draw state names from a grab bag.

3. Place research and other materials where they can be shared. Pass out **The Great State of ____** reproducible page to each group and have a volunteer read the directions aloud. Explain that students will work together to research the necessary information.

4. When all the teams are finished, encourage the Reporters to share their findings. Was there any information they couldn't locate? If so, help groups research further.

5. Continue the activity until information is collected on all 50 states. Then bind the sheets together and leave them in your class social studies center as a reference book.

Focus on Cooperation Ask students to evaluate how successful they were at using **Cooperation Skills** during this activity. Do they feel that they used each skill "always," "most of the time," or "seldom"?

Name_____ Date_____

Name_____

Name_____

The Great State of_____

Work together to follow these instructions:

1. Write the name of your state on the first line.
2. Research to find out the state facts.
3. Fill in the blanks with your answers.
4. Draw pictures to show the state bird, flower, and tree.

Name of the state:_____

State Capital:_____

Nickname:_____

The State Flower is the _____.

The State Bird is the _____.

The State Tree is the _____.

Write a ✔
Today our group practiced
sharing materials_____
sharing ideas _____
speaking quietly_____

Time Line Mix-Ups

Goals:
- Students will make a time line showing notable events in baseball history.
- Students will practice sharing materials and speaking politely.

Suggested number of students in each group: 3
Suggested jobs: Checker, Booster, Organizer

What Each Team Needs:
scissors
glue
12" x 18" construction paper
Team-Up Sheet (page 15)
appropriate **Job Sheets** (pages 18-20)
Time Line Mix-Ups reproducible
  (page 87)

What You Do:
1. Introduce the activity by presenting students with a time line like the following:

FIRST GRADE	SECOND GRADE	THIRD GRADE
1991	1992	1993

Ask what the time line shows. Why are time lines helpful? Challenge children to suggest other events that might be presented in a time line.

2. Assign students to groups of three and give each a **Time Line Mix-Ups** reproducible page. Explain that an event in baseball history is noted in each box, but the events are out of order. Ask a volunteer to read aloud the directions for making a time line. Alert students to the clue in each box—either a year or the words "before" or "after."

3. Set up materials in a central work area and distribute copies of the **Team-Up Sheet** and the appropriate **Job Sheets** for students to complete.

4. Now invite groups to follow the directions to make their baseball time lines. Display the completed time lines so teams can compare their results.

Focus on Cooperation Suggest that students talk about how successful they were at speaking politely. Ask them to give examples. Did any problems arise over the sharing of materials? How might students work together to prevent this kind of problem from happening again?

Time Line Mix-Ups

Can you un-mix the cards to make a baseball history time line?

Work together to follow these instructions:
1. Cut out the time-line cards.
2. Start with the earliest year and paste the cards in order of time on construction paper.

Write a ✔
Today our group practiced
sharing materials_____
speaking kindly _____
speaking politely _____

Hank Aaron broke the home run record with 715 home runs in 1974.	Mickey Mantle scored 94 home runs in 1960, a record for switch-hitters.
Jackie Robinson was voted the Most Valuable Player in 1949.	One year before Jackie Robinson was MVP, Roy Campanella came to play for the Dodgers.
About 14 years after Honus Wagner played, Cy Young ended his career.	Honus Wagner was a top all-around player in 1897.
Casey Stengel was manager of the New York Mets in 1962.	Babe Ruth broke home run records in 1935 with home run number 714.

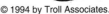

Tales They Told

Goals:
▪ Students will learn about early Native American picture symbols and create picture symbols of their own.
▪ Students will practice sharing ideas, being good listeners, and speaking quietly.

| Friends | go | to their home | by the lake |

Suggested number of students in each group: 3
Suggested jobs: Guide, Recorder, Checker

What Each Team Needs:
crayons/markers
drawing paper
Team-Up Sheet (page 15)
appropriate **Job Sheets** (pages 16-18)

What You Do:
1. Draw the following symbols on the chalkboard:

Challenge students to suggest meanings for each:

home   lake   go   friends

Explain that before written language, some Native American tribes used symbols marked on buffalo hides to record important events.

2. Explain that children will use the symbols they have learned and create their own to describe an event or tell a story. Encourage students to experiment with different combinations of simple symbols.

3. Discuss the different jobs involved:
▪ discussing and creating symbols
▪ drawing the symbols to tell a story
▪ adding new symbols as necessary
▪ revising and editing the picture story

4. Provide students with art materials and copies of the **Team-Up Sheet** and the appropriate **Job Sheets** to complete.

5. Display students' picture stories. Allow time for children to review and try to read each other's work.

Focus on Cooperation Ask students to discuss why it was important to be able to talk to each other during this activity. Did working together stimulate creativity in coming up with symbols? Did talking to each other help the exchange of ideas?

Let's Take a Trip

Goals:
▪ Students will learn about Washington, D.C., by planning an imaginary tour of the city.
▪ Students will practice asking questions, listening to group members, and sharing ideas.

Suggested number of students in each group: 5

Suggested jobs: Guide, Recorder, Checker, Organizer, Reporter

What Each Team Needs:
writing paper
pencils
crayons/markers
resource materials on Washington, D.C., such as travel guides, non-fiction books, encyclopedias
Team-Up Sheet (page 15)
appropriate **Job Sheets** (pages 16, 17, 18, 20, and 21)

What You Do:
1. Display a map of the United States. Help children locate Washington, D.C. Explain that Washington, D.C. is an enormously popular place to visit because there are so many interesting sights to visit and things to see. Challenge children to name famous D.C. landmarks they might know.

2. Divide the class into groups of five and display resource materials. Explain that groups will pretend to be "tour guides" and plan a tour of Washington, D.C., by creating a collection of pictures with notes that describe each place to visit and sight to see.

3. Encourage children to figure out the different jobs involved:
▪ choosing places to visit
▪ drawing a picture of each place
▪ writing notes about the place
▪ revising and editing each other's writings
▪ helping the Reporter prepare an oral report

4. Then pass out copies of the **Team-Up Sheet** and the appropriate **Job Sheets** and arrange materials where they can be shared.

5. When ready, set aside time for Reporters to show pictures and present the group's work as a guided tour through Washington, D.C.

Focus on Cooperation Talk about how asking questions and being good listeners go together. Discuss why fielding questions was helpful for finding out information.

Patchwork Quilt

Goals:
▪ Students will use graph-paper squares to create a paper patchwork quilt.
▪ Students will practice sharing materials, sharing ideas, giving compliments.

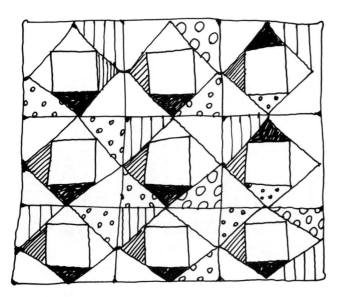

Suggested number of students in each group: 4
Suggested jobs: Guide, Checker, Booster, Organizer

What You Need:
samples or illustrations of patchwork quilts

What Each Team Needs:
1/4" graph paper cut into 3" x 3" squares
markers, colored pencils, or crayons
tape
Team-Up Sheet (page 15)
appropriate **Job Sheets** (pages 16, 18, 19, and 20)

What You Do:
1. Show the children a quilt or an illustration of one made up of squares of material. Tell children that quilt making is a very old art. In Colonial times women would gather in "sewing bees" and work together to create a quilt. Explain that through the years popular designs were copied and re-created. Show examples, if available.

2. Gather children and demonstrate how to make a paper quilt square by coloring in graph-paper squares to form a repeated design or pattern. Then show how to tape two squares on the reverse sides of the paper. Explain that 9, 12, 16, or 20 is a good number of squares to make the "quilt."

3. Now invite children to work in teams to make their own paper quilts. Divide the class into groups of four and distribute copies of the **Team-Up Sheet** and the appropriate **Job Sheets** for students to complete. Place materials where they can be shared.

4. Suggest that students decide upon a theme for their quilts, such as pets, sports, flowers, and so on. Then give students time to create their designs and combine their squares to make their quilts.

5. Invite groups to share their completed quilts with the class. Which parts did each member work on? Could they see why working together helped create the quilt more quickly?

Focus on Cooperation Evaluate with the groups how well they were able to stay on task during this activity. If they had problems, what distractions diverted their attention? How can distractions be avoided?

Squiggles

Goals:
- Students will exercise their imaginations by interpreting "squiggles."
- Students will practice sharing ideas and feelings, being good listeners, and speaking politely.

Suggested number of students in each group: 3
Suggested jobs: Guide, Booster, Organizer

What Each Team Needs:
unlined index cards
markers
Team-Up Sheet (page 15)
appropriate **Job Sheets** (pages 16, 19, and 20)
Squiggles reproducibles (page 92)

What You Do:
1. Draw the following on the chalkboard:

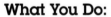

Challenge students to study the drawing and give ideas about what it might be (a cat behind a table, two tents on an empty field, two mountains in the distance, for example). What does this example tell them? Guide students to realize that people can interpret what they see differently.

2. Then divide students in groups of three. Give each child a copy of the **Squiggles** reproducible page and have the directions read aloud. Explain that teammates will brainstorm ideas about the art and then choose several ideas to write in the spaces below each squiggle.

3. Before they begin, pass out copies of the **Team-Up Sheet** and the appropriate **Job Sheets** and place materials in a central work area.

4. After groups complete the first half, draw their attention to the second part of the activity, asking students to make several squiggle drawings of their own for teammates to interpret. Provide index cards and challenge students to work creatively to complete their squiggles.

5. Pause to compliment students on the way they are cooperating and talking in quiet voices.

Focus on Cooperation Ask the different groups to compare how they divided the tasks involved in this activity. Were there any discrepancies? How were they solved?

Name_____ Date_____

Name_____

Name_____

Squiggles

Are these just funny little squiggles or are they something else?
What could they be? Use your imagination to figure them out.

Directions:

1. Think about each squiggle drawing. Share your
   ideas and write three guesses.
2. Then make some squiggle drawings of your own and
   let your teammates guess what they might be.

Write a ✔
Today our group practiced
sharing ideas _____
sharing feelings _____
speaking politely _____

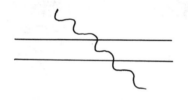

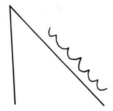

_____

_____

_____

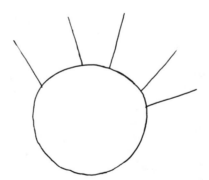

_____

_____

_____

A Is for Artist

Goals:
- **Students will create still-life montages.**
- **Students will practice sharing ideas and materials and giving compliments.**

Suggested number of students in each group: 4

Note: Because of the nature of this activity, the traditional cooperative learning roles are not necessary.

What Each Team Needs:
drawing paper
crayons/markers
pastels
watercolors
paintbrushes
a still-life model like a bowl of fruit
tape

What You Do:

1. Let children work in groups of four. Present children with different art materials: watercolors and brushes, pastels, markers, crayons. Tell children that as artists, they will be able to choose which medium to use.

2. Next, display a reproduction of a still-life painting or discuss what "still-life" means in art (an arrangement of objects, such as fruit in bowl or flowers in vase). Invite students to share their experiences seeing or creating still-life pictures. Point out that it is common practice in art classes to have everyone draw the same object. Ask students to predict whether or not the drawings would be exactly alike.

3. Now display a still-life model (a bowl of fruit, for example) for children to draw. Explain that each group member will create the still-life drawing using a different medium. After, their pictures will be grouped to form a montage.

4. Arrange materials for everyone to use. Encourage teammates to talk about their ideas and to give each other help as needed.

5. When the still-life drawings are dry, instruct students to tape them together on their reverse sides. Then let teams study each montage and compare and contrast the different still-life pictures used to create it.

Focus on Cooperation Distribute index cards and ask students to write compliments they might have given or received during this activity.

Place and Trace Patterns

Goals:
- Students will use one simple pattern to create a repeated design.
- Students will practice taking turns, sharing materials, and speaking quietly.

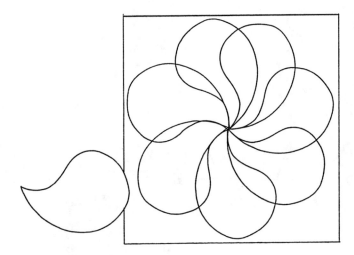

Suggested number of students in each group: 3
Suggested jobs: Checker, Booster, Organizer

What Each Team Needs:
scissors
oaktag
glue
pencils, colored pencils, or crayons
drawing paper
Team-Up Sheet (page 15)
appropriate **Job Sheets** (pages 18-20)
Place and Trace Patterns reproducible
  (page 95)

What You Do:
1. Invite students to name places where they have seen intricate patterns (wallpaper, wrapping paper, floor tiles, museum art work, for example).

2. Divide the class into groups of three. Tell children they will work with their teams to create intricate repeated designs using simple patterns.

Demonstrate the following steps:
- Cut out one shape from the **Place and Trace Patterns** reproducible page.
- Trace it onto oaktag and cut it out to make a template.
- Draw a black dot in the center of the drawing paper.
- Place the point of the shape on the dot and trace the pattern with a pencil.
- Move the shape very slightly with the point remaining on the dot and trace it again. Repeat until you have completed a circle of shapes creating a design.
- Color in the design.

3. To help children get started, pass out the **Team-Up Sheet** and the appropriate **Job Sheets** to fill out.

4. Place materials where they can be shared and give a **Place and Trace Patterns** reproducible page to each group. Explain that children will take turns helping each other use the shapes to make the designs.

5. Invite teams to color in their repeated pattern designs or to trade designs with other teams. Use the designs to decorate the classroom or bind them together to create an interesting book of designs.

Focus on Cooperation Ask students if any sharing problems arose. If so, ask teams to role-play what happened. Invite the class to discuss how each problem could have been solved.

Place and Trace Patterns

These simple shapes can be used to make terrific designs.
Try it together and see.

1. Cut out each shape.
2. Trace the shapes to make oaktag templates.
3. Use the oaktag templates to make a repeated design.

Shiny Shape Mobiles

Goals:
▪ Students will use shapes and foil to create mobiles.
▪ Students will practice taking turns, sharing materials, and exchanging ideas.

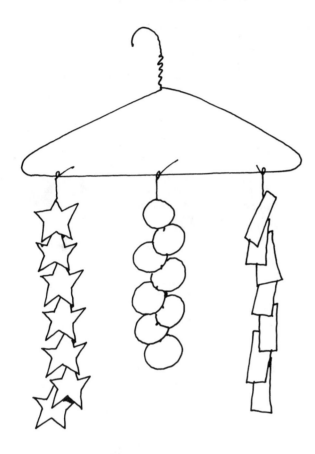

Suggested number of students in each group: 4
Suggested jobs: Guide, Checker, Booster, Organizer

What Each Team Needs:
scissors
white glue
oaktag
hole puncher
string
wire hanger
tape
Team-Up Sheet (page 15)
appropriate **Job Sheets** (pages 16, 18, 19, and 20)

What You Do:
1. Recall with children that a mobile is a hanging sculpture that moves and balances. Tell children that by using simple shapes and their imaginations, they can create beautiful mobiles.

2. Arrange children in groups of four. Ask students to name the different shapes they might want to use and to jot them down. Lay out materials for easy access.

3. Distribute copies of the **Team-Up Sheet** and the appropriate **Job Sheets** for them to complete.

4. Now help groups follow these steps in making their mobiles:
▪ Cut out various shapes from oaktag.
▪ Use them as a pattern to make several more cutouts of the same shape.
▪ Cover the shapes with aluminum foil.
▪ Use tape to attach several like shapes in a series.
▪ Use the hole puncher to make a hole at the top of each shape series.
▪ Attach the shape with string to the hanger.

5. Invite groups to present their mobiles. Then display them around the room.

Focus on Cooperation Review the list of **Cooperation Skills** (see page 13) and ask students to evaluate which skills were most important for this activity.